LOST YEARS

Memories of my homeland

Lost Years
Memories of my homeland
By Margarete G. Mueller
©2010 by LMSEDIT
Cover photo ©2010 by LMSEDIT

PUBLISHED BY LMSEDIT
BOX 1963, CORNWALL, ONTARIO, CANADA K6H 6N7

ISBN 978-1-926650-03-6

Die Erinnerung ist das einzige Paradies,
woraus wir nicht vertrieben werden können.

Memory is the only paradise
from where we cannot be expelled.

(Jean Paul)

Land der dunklen Wälder
Und kristallnen Seen,
Über weite Felder
Lichte Wunder geh'n.

Heimat, wohlgeborgen
Zwischen Strand und Strom,
Blühe heut und morgen
Unterm Friedensdom[1].

My homeland was in *Ostpreussen*[2] which is now generally referred to as the "former East Prussia." You will not find this region on any current map, because it ceased to exist in 1945. *Ostpreussen* became, in effect, just another silent victim of a senseless war.

But *Ostpreussen* will always live in my memory. This land of dark forests and crystal lakes remains in my heart to this day, even though sixty years have gone by since I last saw my homeland.

All the horrors of the war, the chaos and the expulsion that followed, and the almost five years that I was kept imprisoned in Russia will never destroy the beautiful images in my mind's eye.

I wrote this book to share my memories of childhood, hardship, survival, hope and love with my children and grandchildren. Perhaps one day their curiosity will be aroused and then I hope that my book will give them a better understanding of what my life was like.

I remember hearing as a child, that it was the capacity to have sensitivity for the pain and sorrow of others that made us human, and my experiences have taught me how very important it is to care about each other as fellow human beings. This is the true essence of my *Lost Years*.

I believe that you must have an understanding of the past to make sense of the present. We are truly the sum of all our experiences, good and bad. Everything that I have experienced has made me the person I am today. Everything that I am, I pass on to future generations. This is the real legacy that I pass on to my children and grandchildren.

With love,

Mom (Oma)

This book is dedicated to that wonderful nurse in Russia, who gave me the will to live, to fight the odds when there was very little to live for. "You must get well so that you can go home again, *Margaretta!* You don't want to be buried here, in Russia, do you?" Her words had given me strength then.

Perhaps she already knew then, that one day I would somehow write this story. She had helped me to survive and she is the inspiration behind this book.

CHANGED NAMES

I was born in 1927 in *Pregelswalde³,* which was part of *Wehlau⁴,* situated in the former East Prussia. At that time, this small village was home to approximately seven hundred and fifty people. *Pregelswalde* was about thirty kilometers from the former city of *Königsberg⁵.*

Today, *Pregelswalde* is known as *Zarec'e, Wehlau* is known as *Snamensk* and *Königsberg* is known as *Kaliningrad.* Looking at a current map, how many people would know that these places once had German names? How many people know that East Prussia once existed?

I lived in *Imten* until I was seventeen years old. Now over sixty years have passed since I last saw this small village not far from *Pregelswalde.* As far as I know, *Imten* was never given a Russian name. Perhaps this village of some three hundred souls was considered too small, too insignificant an area.

With the exception of my Aunt Gretchen, our family did not own a camera, and most of the photographs that we had were lost during the war, so I can only describe my home town from memory and from the few photos that were salvaged.

Someone recently gave me a photo of this area as it looks today, showing the only remaining house. The picture looks sad and forlorn to me, because I have very different memories of how this village once looked. What happened to all the houses? What happened to all the villagers?

MY FATHER

You might be interested to know that I was raised by my grand-parents and never knew my own father. This is not so unusual today, but when I was a girl, this void in my life haunted me all the time. I was so ashamed of the fact that I did not have a "real" father, that I kept it a secret until I was about thirty years old. It is odd how such a little detail can influence your life so much.

Only later would I learn that my paternal grandfather was a teacher in *Pregelswalde* and that as a child, my mother had attended school with my father. This father I never knew came from quite a large family. He had five brothers and six sisters. One child died at a very young age. All the children in this family learned a trade and my father's choice was to become a brick layer.

This is unfortunately all I know of my father's family. I wish I knew more, for myself and also for my children and grandchildren. My biological father has always been an enigma to me; a missing link, a mystery that may never be solved. Even the word "father" seems so strange to my ears, because he was never a part of our family.

Sixty years ago it was still considered a scandal to have a child out of wedlock and this influenced my decision not to make too many enquiries about my father. Perhaps I also thought it would hurt my mother if I asked a lot of questions. But of course the questions were always very close to my heart and I regret today that I did not probe a little more. It would have been nice to know what he looked like and what sort of man he was.

There were many occasions in my childhood when I was reminded that I was born out of wedlock and the insensitive remarks from teachers and employers made my life miserable at times.

I often wondered what it was like to have a father. Would my mother have been different, if she had had a husband? Someone to share her life, her joys and sorrows? Would my life have been any different, if I had had a father?

1928 TO 1934

When I was about a year old, I moved with my maternal grandparents, my Aunt Hanna and her husband from *Pregelswalde* to *Imten.* I never learned why they moved but I imagine they wanted to start a new life away from *Pregelswalde*, and away from scandal and gossip.

Due to these and other circumstances, I would be separated from Mother for six years. Meanwhile, Mother had a position in *Romau*, working on a small estate about four kilometres away. Opportunities for family visits would be rare.

Imten was a small village of about three hundred people, situated six kilometers from *Tapiau* and consisted of several large estate farms, all of them very neat and orderly. Prussians are said to have an obsession with neatness and orderliness. These attributed characteristics may be stereotypical, but I believe that there is usually some truth in stereotypes.

My family worked on the Urban Estate and the Böhnke, Prack, Perl, Henze, Rode and Lorenz families were our neighbours. Farmer Henze and Farmer Lorenz were relatives of my father. They owned large areas of farmland which were planted with barley, corn, wheat, oats, and potatoes.

Sometimes, when my mind drifts back to those peaceful days, I wonder what happened to the people of *Imten* and other East Prussian towns and villages just like *Imten*. Old maps of the former East Prussia are dotted with hundreds of little towns.

I know that the magnificent estates in East Prussia were mostly destroyed by the invading Russian army, or left to ruin in the post-war years, but what happened to all the people that lived in East Prussia?

Imten had one small, very well-kept inn, where villagers could also purchase a few essential goods. This was handy, since it was not always convenient to make the six-kilometre trip to *Tapiau*.

Although a small village, *Imten* had its own town-hall, which also served as our community center and home to our town nurse. Since we did not have a hospital nearby, our nurse was very important to us. There were always times when home remedies were not sufficient.

My Uncle Otto, Aunt Hanna's husband, worked for Farmer Urban from 1928 to 1942. In 1942, my uncle would be drafted into the army and I would never see him again until 1950. My mother would return to live with us in 1934 and she would also work for Farmer Urban until 1945. That is, until the *Vertreibung* changed everything.

For readers who are not familiar with the German language, I must explain that the word "Vertreibung" is a derivative of the verb "treiben" which means to drive or drive out. The usual English translation for *Vertreibung* is "expulsion" but it does not really convey the true horror of that word and what it means to be driven away from your homeland forever.

The word "expulsion" cannot describe how Prussian families were torn apart and how a way of life would simply vanish for millions of people. An entire culture would disappear. As if East Prussia had never really existed.

When I was a young girl, I would never have imagined that German would not be the first language of my own children and grandchildren or great grand-children. How could I believe that a language and culture taken for granted by Mother, Grandmother and the generations before them would be lost for always?

My Aunt Frieda and Uncle Albert (Mother's brother) lived in *Zopen*, a small village about four kilometres from *Pregelswalde*. My Uncle Gustav and Aunt Auguste lived across the street from us in a small house and of course Aunt Hanna and Uncle Otto lived together with us. It was nice to have so many relatives living close by and I thought it would always remain that way.

About six kilometres north-east of *Imten,* the town of *Tapiau* was situated. This was where we purchased goods which were not available in our village.

Every morning, a train consisting of a locomotive and two or three cars, would arrive. This train came from *Friedland*[6] which was located approximately fifteen kilometres south of *Imten*. Villagers from *Imten* would catch this train to go shopping or do other errands in *Tapiau.* This little train was our only means of transportation, other than travelling by bicycle or horse and wagon.

Grandmother and I would take the *Friedland* train whenever we wanted to go to the *Wochenmarkt* to buy items that were not available in *Imten*. She had a large black shopping bag for these excursions. It was large enough to carry some flour or sugar and perhaps some apples or a cake from the baker. *Streusselkuchen*, a tasty crumble-cake, and *Americaner,* a mouth-watering chocolate-covered cake would always delight me. We did not have that many sweets those days and cakes were usually reserved for special treats, or for occasions when we had visitors.

Grandmother always brought along a pillow-case, because sometimes her purchases would be too heavy for her black leather shopping bag. We did not have plastic shopping bags then! But with Grandmother's pillow-case, the load could be divided and I could help her to carry at least part of it.

Sometimes we did not wait for the return train to *Imten* and walked the six kilometres back home. The return train arrived only at 7:30 in the evening and Grandmother did not always want to wait until then. But the walk from *Tapiau* to *Imten* could be quite long for a child and grandmother carrying a load of groceries.

THE VILLAGE OF IMTEN

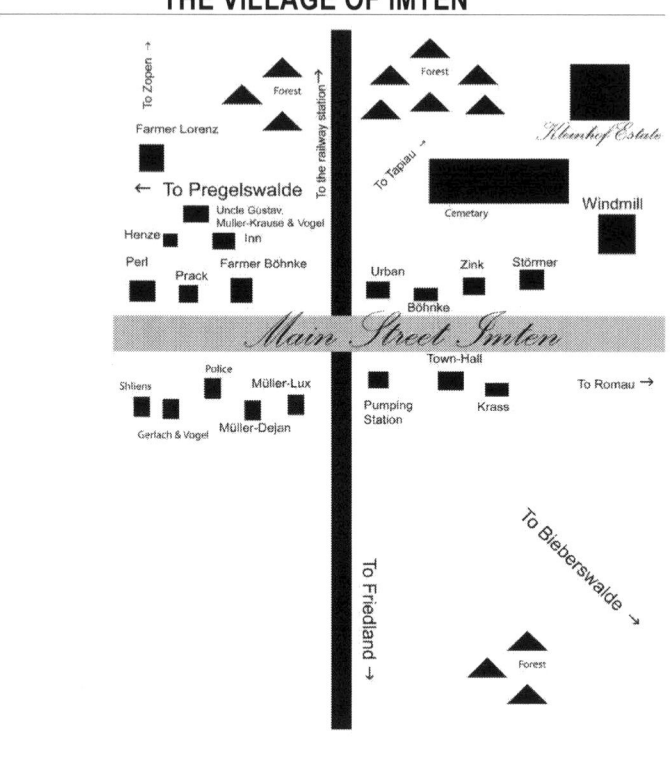

To Zopen ↑

Forest

Farmer Lorenz

← To Pregelswalde

To the railway station ↑

To Tapiau ↗

Forest

Kleinhof Estate

Cemetary

Windmill

Uncle Gustav, Muller-Krause & Vogel

Inn

Henze

Perl   Prack   Farmer Böhnke

Urban   Zink   Störmer

Böhnke

Main Street Imten

Police   Town-Hall

Shliens   Müller-Lux   To Romau →

Gerlach & Vogel   Müller-Dejan   Pumping Station   Krass

To Friedland ↓

To Bieberswalde ↗

Forest

UNCLE KARL'S WEDDING

The photograph on the previous page was taken on the occasion of my Uncle Karl's wedding. Uncle Karl is sitting in the front row beside his bride Anna. Uncle Gustav is in the third row, third from the right. To his left is his wife, my Aunt Auguste. Aunt Hanna is in the back row, first from the left. Uncle Albert can be seen in the back third row, first from the right.

Uncle Albert was my favourite uncle and always seemed to understand me when no one else did. I remember that in my teens, when I asked Mother if I could cut my hair she simply said:

"No. You will only look sloppy with short hair!"

I wanted so badly to have my hair bobbed short. So many of my friends had cut off their braids in favour of this new "modern" look. A look that of course horrified the older generation! What could I do? There was no getting around Mother.

With a twinkle in his eye, Uncle Albert had suggested that I find him a pair of scissors and he would do the job himself. But then Grandmother stepped in and proclaimed:

"Over my dead body! The hair stays on her head!"

Once Grandmother made a decision, there was no room for compromise. Stubbornness was definitely a family trait!

Mother is absent from this wedding picture and it always amused me to hear how she would exhibit this same family stubbornness when she refused to pose for this important occasion.

It had been arranged that for the wedding dinner Mother would sit beside the young gentleman in the second row; first from the right in the photograph. But Mother did not want to be his dinner date and declined to give any explanation.

Uncompromising as she was, she would not even deign to pose beside him for the photograph, and that was that! No amount of bribing, cajoling or pleading would change her mind.

Wedding or no wedding, she had to have her way. And obviously she did get her way! What a challenge to Grandmother on the day of her son's wedding! Perhaps Mother was more headstrong than Grandmother, after all. Grandmother was forced to give in and Mother's refusal to adapt herself to a little social custom was recorded for all posterity in the family portrait!

I always wondered how the young gentleman felt about Mother's rejection. He does not look very happy in this picture, but everyone seems to have looked rather solemn that day. Even the bride is not smiling. Was it Mother's obstinacy that put a pall on the wedding? Or were weddings in *Ostpreussen* simply more sombre those days?

OUR TWO-ROOM HOME

Aunt Hanna and Uncle Otto had two sons and these boys, Kurt and Fritz, were more like brothers to me than cousins, since we lived in the same house. Until 1940, there were eight of us living under the same roof — Grandmother, Grandfather, Aunt Hanna, Uncle Otto, my cousins Kurt and Fritz, my mother and myself.

You are probably thinking that it is impossible for eight people to share two rooms, but in the 1930s this was quite a common practice and indeed a very practical arrangement. We pooled our resources and there were certainly enough chores to go around.

When I look back, I wonder how we all managed in our tiny two-room house. Three generations and so very little privacy! But family ties were very strong and there was great comfort in growing up in this supportive atmosphere, where someone was always there when help was needed. In our village, and in our families, loneliness was not possible, simply because we were never alone.

It was not unusual those days to have several generations living together. This arrangement would probably not work for most families today. But I think that in our quest today for freedom and privacy, we have lost something very precious which is not so easily found again. I believe that people were not meant to live in compartments and in isolation from one another, as many do today.

Our home was an old brick house and the roof was covered with moss and it always seemed very cosy and warm to me. Although we had very little material wealth, what we owned was very well-cared for, as if it was understood that our belongings would be handed down to the next generation.

Furniture and bed linen were meant to last a lifetime and were treated with utmost respect. This meant that we were not permitted to sit on the sofa, except when we had company. Beds were meant only for sleeping. This meant that we could not lie down, or even sit on the bed in the day time.

A sense of order and thriftiness were very important to our household. Clothing was never thrown away; it was "altered" and socks were darned and repaired over and over again until the patches looked as though they were part of a pattern.

Our best clothes were only worn on special occasions and would always be carefully packed away afterwards. Old clothes would be worked on and transformed into smaller versions for children, or find new life as rugs or potholders. The wool in old sweaters would be salvaged by rolling it into skeins. This wool could then be used for knitting new scarves or other items of clothing. We would never throw anything out if it was possible to alter or mend it. Cloth was simply too precious.

Having our own sheep was a big advantage for our family because my grandmother was able to spin her own wool. Using her own wool, she would then knit the wool into gloves and socks for us to wear. I did not always appreciate these home-made wool socks, because they tended to be scratchy.

Our streets were not crowded with fast-food restaurants and shopping centers that we see everywhere today and we certainly did not have the money to buy frivolous items.

I am sitting on Grandmother's lap. My grandparents are wearing their best clothes, because we were attending the wedding of Uncle Karl.

Grandmother looks stern, possibly because her daughter, (my mother) refused to pose in this family photograph.

This picture was taken in Tapiau at the photographer's shop and I am about four years old. Mother and Grandmother had very strict rules about the type of shoes I could wear — no "party shoes" for me! The shoes always seemed to be too tight. My hair was specially braided and then combed out so that I would have waves for that day!

FAMILY LIFE

Uncle Otto was fortunate to have work at the large Urban Estate nearby. Although his earnings were meagre by today's standards, he had pigs, sheep, chickens and a cow of his own and he was also permitted a certain allotment of feed from the estate for his animals. So we had everything we needed to live comfortably.

My grandfather was employed by the town as a *Strassenwerter* and one of his jobs was to maintain the streets in *Imten* and surrounding area. His duties included maintaining the stately old trees in our village; pruning and caring for them. It was very important to preserve the beauty of our village for future generations.

Mother lived and worked in *Romau*, approximately four kilometres away from *Imten*. A short distance today, but not so in 1928 on foot! It was a rare occasion when she was able to come to *Imten*, so we usually walked to visit her there instead.

Working on an estate as a servant, Mother was kept busy taking care of the house as well as minding the chickens, and pigs. Cleaning the pig pens and chicken coups, and working in the field were all part of her duties. Her days were very long, but she never complained about the work.

Once a month, usually a Sunday, Grandfather took me by the hand and we walked the four kilometres, so that I could see my mother. I always looked forward to these visits. They were very special, even though they were very short.

In *Romau*, my mother lived in a small room and we were able to visit for just a couple of hours with her before walking the four kilometres back home again. Mother was always happy to see us and her employers were very kind to me. Working as hard as she did, there was very little time for other diversions.

Grandfather and Grandmother enjoying a Sunday afternoon.

Uncle Otto, on the Urban Estate. He was very fond of horses.

Horses on the Urban Estate.

I did not learn that Mother had considered giving me up for adoption until I was forty years old. How can a mother give up her own child for adoption? If I had known about this as a child, it might have caused me some anguish and perhaps some bitterness, but at the age of forty, I had a different perspective. And now that I am eighty years old, I think I understand why my mother felt the way she did.

The thought of abandoning a child may sound somewhat unnatural today, but we must keep in mind that in the early 1920s, society was extremely harsh on young unwed mothers. Perhaps, in her dilemma at that time, Mother had sought the advice of her employers and as a childless couple, they were very willing to adopt me. No doubt, Mother saw a much brighter future for me there, where I would live in comparative luxury.

But when Grandfather got wind of Mother's idea, he would not hear of it and immediately declared:

"No, the child is our flesh and blood and will stay with us."

Grandfather could be stubborn too. His final decision took precedence over his daughter's predicament and that is why I lived with my grandparents until I was six years old.

Having an out-of-wedlock child was certainly a hardship for my mother and also made it difficult for her to find a husband. But I was always certain that Mother loved me and I have since learned that what bound us together as a family was much stronger than any inconvenience for my mother.

My grandparents were adamant about keeping me in the family and I was very lucky that they felt this way. My family was always very precious to me and I am grateful that I was able to grow up in a loving and nurturing home. The solid foundation I had with

Grandmother and Grandfather later gave me strength in times of need.

I loved my grandfather very much, and still think of him often. Grandfather was a sensitive, gentle man and always knew how to comfort me. One icy winter's day, after leaving my mother's room in *Romau*, my feet were so cold, even though I was wearing thick wool socks. But I was afraid to say anything to Grandfather. In those days, children were not supposed to whimper and complain, so I kept still about this and kept walking.

But on arriving back home in *Imten*, I started to cry, for my feet hurt me so.

"If your feet are frozen, you must put them in cold water immediately!" responded Grandfather, when he found out about my problem. Grandfather was right. He rubbed my feet vigorously and everything was alright again in a short while.

I have so many happy memories of the time I spent with my grandfather. Grandfather was always considerate and gentle with me and I could always go to him for advice. He was also a wonderful story-teller.

Often, he would put me in his wagon and survey the road while teaching me everything he knew about horticulture and the natural wonders around us.

His knowledge of plant material was vast; an accumulation of many years of hands-on experience.

I would feel very special sitting on the wagon among his tools, enjoying the sunshine and observing nature all around me. Then he would park the wagon and I would watch with great interest while Grandfather tended to the maple trees that lined both sides of the street.

In summer, the ditches overflowed with beautiful wildflowers and I felt very close to the earth. I believe that my love of nature came from the hours I spent with Grandfather, watching him at work.

I sometimes wished that my mother could have more time for me. But I understood that the times were hard and she had to work every day to help support our household. Even on Sunday, farm animals had to be looked after, so she did not even really have much time for herself, let alone a young child.

It helped to have Aunt Hanna and Uncle Otto living with us. My cousins Kurt and Fritz sometimes played with me and I had many cousins and other children in the village to play with as well. Though I missed my mother, it was difficult to be really lonely in our village.

Our lives always seemed to harmonize quite well. I do not remember big quarrels or harsh words, let alone shouting or swearing. The times before 1939 were the happiest and most carefree years for me. I felt safe and comfortable within my family and I was blissfully unaware of what lay ahead.

When I was six years old I learned that Mother was finally coming home. What a happy surprise for me! Though I had grown accustomed to her absence, I was overjoyed that she would be coming home to *Imten* to live with the family again. Having Mother in *Imten* meant that I would have a *real* mother, just like other children. I loved Grandmother, but she could never be my mother.

From that time on, Mother worked on the same estate as Uncle Otto. I believe my uncle had been instrumental in helping Mother obtain a position as farm worker on the Urban Estate. Her work was not any easier, but I am sure that it was great comfort for her to be with the family again.

I never heard Mother complain about her work. Every morning, the family would get up at six o'clock, but Mother would already be gone by then. After all, she always had fifty to seventy pigs to feed, as well as chickens and geese to take care of, before hurrying off to work the fields.

This photograph shows me in the second grade, working at my lessons. To save paper, children used chalk pencils and wrote on slate boards.

Uncle Karl and Uncle Otto are constructing a fence, in front of the Müller home. These Müllers were not related to our family, although we shared the same name.

Mother (far right, wearing a polka-dotted apron) with the other farm-workers on the Urban Estate.

Below: Mother (second from the left) enjoying a little rest after working hard in the fields on the Urban Estate.

Much of our family life was centred on the preparation of food. Cooking was Grandmother's department since she had many years of experience and she was in fact official custodian of family recipes and special techniques that had been handed down through several generations.

Grandmother always planned our meals for us. I can still hear Aunt Hanna asking:

"Mother, what should we cook today?" My aunt would not think of preparing a meal without first consulting with Grandmother.

One of our favourite meals was sausages. Every six months, two pigs would be butchered and pickled in salt for six weeks and then smoked. We had a little smoke house not far from our house, so we were able to make our own sausages.

Grandmother always performed the "taste test" while the meat was being prepared, and she also controlled the amount of meat that was stuffed into the sausage casings. She knew exactly how long to cook the sausages before lightly smoking them.

On "sausage days" the aroma of marjoram, an essential herb in the meat mixture, permeated every room. Even today, the scent of this wonderful herb still makes me think of Grandmother's delicious sausages.

The simple life I am trying to describe might sound under-privileged or "deprived" to people who have grown accustomed to the almost limitless variety of food available today, but we thought very differently in the 1930s. Although we did not have the wide assortment of food that is on every supermarket shelf today, we always had enough to eat and we were contented with what was presented at the dinner table.

I do not think that people suffered from boredom in the 1930s. Hard-working people were much too busy to question whether they were "happy" or "having fun". So they did not desperately seek stimulation elsewhere. In my own family, we entertained ourselves at home by telling stories, singing songs or reading. We could not imagine how life could be otherwise and we never asked ourselves whether we were "having fun".

Debt and borrowing money were foreign terms to us. We did not buy anything if we did not have the money. We simply saved our money until we had enough to buy what we needed. Perhaps I should emphasise that we bought only what we needed, not necessarily what we wanted. But I think there is a danger in wanting to satisfy every craving and desire.

Making things "from scratch" and producing most of our own food allowed us to be very self-sufficient and there is great satisfaction and pride in knowing that you can take care of yourself and your family.

Accepting charity was rare because people had too much pride to admit to what would at that time be considered as failure. Perhaps a lack of self-reliance or an inability to prepare adequately for life is a form of failure in some instances. In any case, charity or what we would probably refer to as "social assistance" was reserved only for the truly needy or the old and helpless.

There was an elderly widow in our village and she was the only really needy person that I knew during my childhood. Although she was not directly related to me, I always called her my "other grandmother".

Our small village was actually like an extended family and so it was inconceivable that she would be abandoned to fend for herself. I believe that a neighbourhood, like a garden, is a reflection of our personalities and I am proud that most villagers in *Imten* felt responsible for the widow's well-being and helped her in different ways. Some brought her food or milk. Others helped with chores or repairs. She was not alone, because she mattered to her neighbours.

This picture was taken on one of Aunt Gretchen's visits. My cousins, Erna and Kurt don't look all that thrilled, but I was very happy that day in my sailor outfit!

EVENINGS IN IMTEN

There were no credit cards those days, so I don't know how long Mother had to save her *Pfennige* in order to buy a little *Volksempfanger*, which was a modest and inexpensive radio. But it was a small miracle and a great pleasure to hear music and listen to the news on the radio back in the 1930s.

The kind of "packaged" entertainment we have today was not available to us then, so our little *Volksempfänger* was a real luxury for us. Having a radio was especially delightful in the wintertime because evenings in East Prussia were very long. It was already dark at three o'clock in the afternoon.

In the wintertime, it was customary for us to have our evening meal at five or six o'clock at the latest. After we had eaten and cleared away the dishes, Aunt Hanna would mend clothing and Grandmother would sit at her spinning wheel, making wool and we would also listen to the radio.

Sometimes Grandfather would tell stories of what was for him the "last war" — World War I. He would then take out his *Soldbuch*, his "pay book" and look over all the entries made during his time as a soldier. These entries would jog his memory, and he would entertain us with his many interesting anecdotes.

I was captivated by his stories and tried to visualize what life must have been like when he was younger. It seemed like ancient history to me at the time; a mysterious bygone era. But fascinating for me, just the same.

We don't have enough storytellers today. Perhaps the younger generations no longer have the patience to listen to the tales of older people and bygone times. Perhaps the entertainment industry has deadened their curiosity about the past.

Today, many children seem to be excessively stimulated from every direction. It is not surprising to me that many children suffer from various degrees of "attention deficit disorder."

But maybe one day, the children of today will miss their connection to their past, and wonder about what came before. Who were there grandparents and great-grandparents? How did they live? Perhaps they will learn to focus and listen more closely then.

CHRISTMAS

Christmas was always a time of wonder and excitement for me. On this occasion, Mother's employer would present her with a large bowl filled with cookies and marzipan. Aunt Hanna would also bake special cookies and cakes at this time, so the tantalizing scent of cinnamon and allspice was everywhere. It seemed like the whole village was alive with *Pfefferkuchen* — a delicious gingerbread!

But these Christmas treats were never meant to be devoured at once and Grandmother always made sure that our spicy cookies and cakes were carefully divided and put away, so that they would last several months.

As for presents, we did not receive the mountains of toys that seem to be the norm today. At the most, we would get two presents and these were most often something to wear, or something that we needed for school.

Our Christmas tree would be cut only one or two days before, so that it was still very fresh for that special evening. On Christmas Eve, it would be ceremoniously decorated, and then the wonderful evergreen fragrance would fill the house.

Although we did not have videos, DVDs and television to entertain us, our house was very cosy and warm and we sang Christmas songs long into the night.

A German Christmas Carol

O du fröhliche,
O du selige,
Gnadenbringende Weihnachtszeit.
Christ ist erschienen,
Uns zu versühnen,
Freue, freue dich, o Christenheit.

A rough translation:

Oh, how joyfully,
Oh, how merrily
Christmas comes with its grace divine
Grace again is beaming
Christ the world redeeming;
Hail, ye Christians,
Hail the joyous Christmas time.

Here I am celebrating Christmas with Aunt Gretchen's family. I am standing beside the Christmas tree. Aunt Gretchen is on the far right and Aunt Gerda is sitting in front of me.

A visit from Königsberg. Grandfather (front, left side) was very close to his brother Hans, who is sitting to the right. Uncle Karl (Grandfather's son) is standing behind them. The photo shows the blacksmith's section of the house in which we lived.

I am standing in front of the Bibergraben, near our home. Imten was an idyllic place to grow up.

1939

This seemed to be a year of bad omens and it was an especially sad year for our family because Grandfather suffered a stroke in February. The stroke paralyzed him on one side and he became quite helpless. It was a tragedy for a man who loved his work and had been so active all his life.

He died in August and would have been 70 years old on September 1, 1939. Sadly, he had been retired for only five years, so he did not have much opportunity for relaxation in his life.

His brother Hans had died six months before in *Königsberg*, and this too, had depressed Grandfather during those final months, and may have been a contributing factor in his own death.

Then, on September 3, Britain and France declared war on Germany. *How will this war affect us?* Naively I had wondered about the consequences of war on that fateful day. I could not foresee how the peace and innocence I grew up with would be shattered. Our lives would never be the same again.

Changes came immediately. A rationing system was soon implemented and food could only be purchased with ration cards. For us, it meant that we could not keep all the milk from our one cow, and from then on, we would be obliged to share our milk with the community. We understood the need for rationing, yet it was difficult to feed a large family properly on this rationing system.

Pigs, and chickens, and all farm animals in our district were carefully counted and allowances were strictly calculated and enforced. For us, this meant that from now on, we were allowed to butcher just one pig a year. This wasn't much food for a large family.

But hard times can foster ingenuity in some people and Uncle Otto found a method for circumventing these new restrictions. At least a little. His solution was to butcher not just one pig, but two. He would quietly butcher one pig just after midnight, when everyone was asleep, and the second one the next day.

This was riskier than it sounds. Those who chose not to comply with the law had to proceed with extreme caution, if they did not want to get caught "hoarding" because punishment for hoarding was quite severe.

I remember when my cousin Kurt went into the pantry where the meat was laid out. He was curious as all boys are and was obviously surprised to see that there were two pigs' heads on the shelf. We were all so afraid that he would inadvertently say something to someone, and get my uncle into trouble. It was mandatory that we keep my uncle's actions a family secret.

When inspectors came to count our animals, we would always say we had one less pig than what we actually had. This was common practice in our village, although no one talked about it with their neighbours. Even with this little "trick" it was still difficult for a family of eight, but we managed by dividing our own share very carefully. Grandmother had lived through the First World War and she knew how to take care of her family.

GRANDMOTHER

In 1939 I was twelve years old and Grandmother did not waste much time letting me know that I was now old enough to help with the household work.

My chores included washing dishes, which was a far more complex task than it is today. We did not have running water in our house, so I would first have to pump the water from a common well which was about three hundred meters from our house. The kitchen had a large container for water that we would have to re-fill every couple of days.

I would carry a special yoke on my shoulders, with a bucket attached to each end to fetch the water. Though I was a fairly strong girl, the water was very heavy.

Because water was so precious, and washing so time consuming, clothes were washed only once a month. Laundry days were long and arduous!

On "bath days" I would fill a large tub with water that had been heated in a large kettle on the stove. Each member of the family would take turn bathing in this tub, and the water would have to last for all of the family.

Feeding the twenty or so chickens and taking care of the chicken coup also became part of my daily routine. The rabbits also had to be fed every day and I would gather suitable plants from the ditches along the road.

I was also in charge of weeding the flower garden and I enjoyed this task tremendously because I liked to be outdoors. We had quite a selection of asters, dahlias and peonies in our flower bed. Every summer, our yard exploded with colour.

To this day, I still prefer outdoor work to house work. But as a young girl, I could not select the chores I preferred. And like many young girls, sometimes I did not feel like doing certain household chores. I remember once when Grandmother asked me to sweep out the pantry, I grumbled:

"Why do *I* always have to do that?"

"Oh, so you don't want to work? A young girl with so much energy? Then I will just have to do it myself!" responded Grandmother.

She was a master of psychological warfare, and Grandmother meant what she said. I was alarmed by her reaction to my somewhat defiant outburst and felt very guilty about what I had said.

"I'm sorry, Grandmother, let me do this." I said quickly as I gently coaxed the broom from her hand.

I loved and respected my Grandmother very much. She was seventy years old and I did not want to hurt or upset her. Especially now that Grandfather was gone.

When I was twelve years old, Grandmother expected me to help with many domestic chores. My cousin Kurt still had a little "freedom."

Grandmother was the matriarch in the family. After Grandfather had passed away, it was understood that Grandmother would assume all responsibility for the household. All important decisions were now made by her and they were generally accepted without opposition by her daughters and son-in-law.

I remember one evening when the family discussed whether our potatoes should be hand-harvested or machine-harvested. The pros and cons were debated and carefully evaluated by the adults in the family. Grandmother preferred hand-harvesting to machine-harvesting and she had very strong arguments in favour of this old-fashioned method.

We always grew our own potatoes and Grandmother took pride in harvesting and storing them properly. They were, after all, an essential component of our diet. Other crops, such as grain feed for the chickens and pigs, could be more easily obtained from the estate where Mother and Uncle Otto worked, and these actually constituted what we would call a "pay package" today.

Grandmother maintained that hand-harvesting was better. She was afraid that with machine-harvesting, some potatoes would be damaged or left in the soil and forgotten. You see, every potato was precious to us.

Waste, in whatever form, or in whatever minute amount, was just not tolerated. This philosophy of frugality comes from people who have not forgotten what it is like to be hungry.

Uncle Otto would have been able to harvest the entire crop of potatoes in less than two days with the harvester that he was permitted to borrow from his employer. But Grandmother was adamant about how *our* harvesting should be done, even though this meant fourteen days of hard work, not just for our family but also for other relatives who would come to help us gather the potatoes.

Although past the age of "retirement" Grandmother still "pulled her own weight" and always assisted at harvest time, so she was very knowledgeable about the process.

I did not always have to help immediately with the harvesting, because Grandmother preferred that I stay home and cook the mid-day meal and take care of household tasks while the rest of the family was out in the field. But I was expected to help out in the afternoon, gathering up the potatoes that had been harvested in the morning. The rows of potatoes were quite long, so this took some time to do.

For harvesting, as with all tasks, there was a definite procedure to follow. First the largest potatoes were collected. These were the potatoes for our normal requirements. Then we would collect the seed potatoes, which would be immediately removed and carefully packed away in trenches for the upcoming year. As an added protection, they would be covered with straw.

The trenches were about a meter deep, two to three meters wide and six meters long. These potatoes had to withstand the cold East Prussian winters, where temperatures sometimes dropped to 30° Celsius! Proper harvesting and storage procedures were very important, since potatoes were our major source of food and preparations always had to be made for the next planting year.

Finally, we would gather up the smaller potatoes for the pigs. Nothing was wasted and this was why Grandmother did not like the harvesting machine. A machine could never replace the thoroughness and precision of a human being, she thought.

Grandmother and Aunt Hanna are visiting Grandfather's grave. It was Grandmother's wish to be buried beside Grandfather, when her time came.

MY OTHER "GRANDMOTHER"

There was another grandmother in the village, where I would deliver milk every two days. She was actually Uncle Otto's grandmother. Her husband had worked on a neighbouring estate and this employer provided free milk to the elderly widow, who had very little income.

She lived about one kilometre away from us. In the summer it was a pleasant walk but the winter could be so cold and dreary.

The entrance to her home was usually quite dark because she only had a small petroleum lamp to light up her small room. She was eighty-three years old and not in very good health; I was always afraid that I would find her dead one day.

My worst fears were realized one Sunday morning, when I found her lying in front of her bed. I ran immediately to the town-hall to alert the community nurse. When we returned together, I helped the nurse lift *Oma* to her bed. The thought that I was touching a dead person terrified me.

The funeral was well-attended because the widow had many grandchildren. I think they all hoped to inherit something from the poor grandmother who had so little and this made me very sad. Since she was buried in the same cemetery where my grandfather lay, I tended her grave as well as that of my grandfather.

In those days, family members would regularly maintain the tomb stones of their departed loved ones, raking the area clean and tidy. Every Saturday afternoon, I went to the cemetery to care for Grandfather's grave as well as the grave of my other "Grandmother".

Sometimes I walked and sometimes I would ride my bicycle to the cemetery. It never occurred to me that I would get paid for doing this work. It was just understood, a matter of course; a simple duty that was as natural to me as helping a blind person across the street.

SUMMER HOLIDAYS

I always looked forward to visits from my *Königsberg* relatives. Aunt Gretchen, Aunt Gerda, Uncle Hans, and their father who was in fact Grandfather's brother and was also named Hans, were our connection to the outside world. When they came to see us, our little house would resonate with the intensity of all manner of discussion and gossip for a couple of days.

The visits were always pleasant and they renewed our family ties but they also required a lot of preparation. Grandmother, Mother, Aunt Hanna and I spent many hours cleaning and scrubbing the house down from top to bottom, preparing the meals and baking cakes for our relatives from *Königsberg.* It was very important to our sense of family pride that our house looked neat and polished and that there was enough to eat.

These relatives, compared to my *Imten* relatives, were extra special to me because they came from "the big city" which seemed very far away and exotic to me at that time. In *Königsberg,* Uncle Hans worked as clerk for the railroad and Aunt Gretchen had a job in an office.

By comparison, we were simple "country folk" and probably not very sophisticated in their eyes. At least this is what Grandmother and Aunt Hanna always said. But Aunt Gretchen and Uncle Hans were never condescending and always seemed to be very comfortable at home with us.

These visits were reciprocated when school was over for the summer. Aunt Gretchen, who was also my godmother, always arranged for me to visit her in *Königsberg* for my summer holidays. Perhaps she wanted to show me that the world was much larger than *Imten* and the surrounding villages.

Aunt Gretchen spent a lot of time with me, taking me on long walks, showing me all the interesting sights in *Königsberg.* When we were tired of walking, we would take the streetcar home to Aunt Gerda's lovely apartment.

As City Inspector, Aunt Gerda's husband was able to afford a comfortable four-room apartment in the city and I would also visit her during my stay. This was a very memorable event for me, because their apartment seemed very elegant and luxurious. Their furniture was so beautiful compared to our simple rustic wooden tables and chairs.

Aunt Gerda would then prepare a meal fit for a princess. That is how I felt when I sat down at the dining-room table. She always set the table with a freshly starched white table cloth, fancy china and a centrepiece of flowers. This was very different from what I was used to in my own home, where we sat in the kitchen around a plain and bare wooden table set with our very ordinary dishes.

It was Aunt Gerda who taught me the intricacies of social etiquette and table manners. It was very important to her that I conduct myself like a proper young lady. This emphasis on manners and refinement would have been out of place in our family, but I could see that customs and behaviour were different in *Königsberg* and I paid attention to my aunt.

Some summers, Aunt Gerda and her husband would take me along on their vacation. For six to eight weeks we would stay in *Rauschen*[7], a popular German resort town in those days.

This is a photograph of my beautiful Aunt Gretchen, to whom I am so grateful. A camera was a luxury in those days, and Mother did not have one. Aunt Gretchen was the photographer in the family and took photographs of us whenever she visited. Without her photographs, so many family memories would have been lost. Fortunately, these photographs are among the few family possessions that survived the *Vertreibung*.

Although I could not swim, and always feared the water, I enjoyed the beach tremendously. Watching people in their swim suits and listening to the rush of water intrigued me. My summer holidays with my *Königsberg* were always an adventure for me.

But still I missed my home in *Imten* and when summer vacation was over, I could not wait to see my family and all the old familiar sights in the village. Of course, Grandmother and the rest of the family were also happy to see me again. A separation of two months was a long time in those days.

Aunt Gerda and Aunt Gretchen always tried very hard to convince me that it would be a good idea for me to leave *Imten* and work in *Königsberg* when I was older. They believed that there were more opportunities for me in the city, and this may have been true. If I did not want to be a house-maid or farm worker, I would have to move to *Königsberg* one day. But that day seemed far away in the distant future.

For now I still lived in *Imten* and I loved my little village very much. Although there were so many interesting things to see in *Königsberg* I did not really want to be a "city girl." The forests, my family, and my familiar surroundings meant that much to me. I could not imagine ever wanting to leave my home permanently.

Aunt Hanna always prepared one of my favourite meals — usually dumplings and cabbage soup — for my arrival back home. As an extra surprise, her delicious home-made caramel candy would be displayed in a little plate on the table to celebrate my return and this always made me feel very special, since we did not have this treat every day.

Aunt Hanna was always kind to me. Later, in my teens, when I sometimes came home a little later than I should have, it was Aunt Hanna who opened the door for me. Actually, our front door was never locked. There were no "intruders" or "home invasions" those days, so we had no reason to lock our doors.

But sometimes the door would be hooked from the inside for the evening, and then I would have to knock on the door. On those occasions I would have to have a good explanation ready!

If Mother or Grandmother came to unhook the door I would be out of luck, because they would immediately interrogate me:

"Why are you so late? Your get-together should not have taken that long!"

Since Mother and Grandmother usually fell asleep by nine-thirty at night, I was fortunate when Aunt Hanna would come to my rescue, dashing to the door, before they could wake up.

In any case, I was never really unreasonably late in coming home. My social outings ended at ten o'clock or ten-thirty at the latest and it wasn't even all that dark at that time, because summer days were very long in East Prussia.

Grandmother, Mother and Aunt Hanna each watched me like a hawk throughout my teenage years. I did not always appreciate this because I was reaching the age when I wanted to spread my wings. They always feared for my safety, but they need not have worried so. Those were still such safe times.

1940

This year started off on a sad note for me, because on February 25, my mother gave birth to my sister Helga. I soon realized that her father was in fact my Uncle Otto and I was very upset about this.

What was Mother thinking of? Why has she done this again? Why did she allow herself to be tempted this way? Why had she let this happen? Didn't she care about how this would hurt me?

It seemed to me, that history was repeating itself and I was very unhappy with Mother. I took the matter very personally; this was another disgraceful affair that would cause me problems at school.

Years of being ridiculed for not having a father had made me very sensitive and this new predicament would only compound my troubles. Naturally, I worried about what people would think and say about Mother and about me.

Looking back, I can see now that there were so many opportunities where my mother could meet with Uncle Otto privately, since they both worked on the same estate. Although she always worked very hard, my Aunt Hanna was a somewhat sickly woman and this likely contributed to the sequence of events.

Today, I have a different perspective on this matter and I have learned to realize that there are so many factors that can cloud what some people would believe is a black and white issue. Nothing is quite that simple, and we should never judge people too harshly when we do not fully comprehend the situation. My knowledge of the world and the complexity of human relationships was limited, so I could not really understand the situation then.

I realize now, that my mother had always had to work very hard and took her responsibility as breadwinner very seriously. She had very little time for herself, for friendship or for love.

Perhaps this liaison with her sister's husband, her brother-in-law, was also bound to happen, because so many young men, who would have been her suitors, had already passed away in the First World War. There were few available men of her age in our area.

Perhaps having two children out of wedlock was in fact a conscious decision on her part. Much later, Mother would tell me that she had not wanted to go through life childless. Perhaps then, this was her only chance for motherhood? I will never really know. My mother, like my father, still remains a mystery to me.

Looking back, I can sympathize with Mother and her "dilemma." She did not have the easy accessibility to birth control, which would have protected her, in our more "convenient" era.

Although the betrayal would still have been evident to those close to her, it would not have been quite so obvious and she would not have been "branded" with this unfortunate indiscretion.

The arrival of Helga obviously required us to make adjustments in our household and for a while the tranquility in our home was disrupted. But with time, we all learned to accept the situation. I eventually learned to forgive Mother, and Aunt Hanna learned to forgive her sister and my Uncle Otto. Time really does heal wounds, even very deep wounds.

Perhaps Aunt Hanna, Grandmother, Uncle Otto and Mother also realized that in the final analysis, they all needed each other. What would be served by hating each other, of bearing a grudge or seeking revenge? It would have amounted to only so much wasted energy and they were people who did not waste anything. They needed their energy for other things.

In any case, we all stayed together in spite of this very obvious proof of infidelity, and I can truly say that my Aunt Hanna accepted and treated my sister Helga as if she were her own daughter. It must have been very difficult for Aunt Hanna, but if she had any negative feelings, she kept these to herself. She did not become a bitter woman, as far as I could tell. Family harmony was very important to her. I think the other members of the family felt the same way.

This is a photograph of Mother holding my sister Helga. Looking at this photo now, I wonder what was going through her head at that time. Did she worry about how she would provide for us? Mother always worked very hard and took her responsibility as breadwinner very seriously. She had very little time for herself, but she was always there for us.

It took me a while to adjust to having a new baby sister in our family, but Helga was a pretty little girl and eventually won my heart.

Back row: Grandmother, Aunt Frieda, Mother, me, Aunt Hanna. Front row: Cousin Fritz, Cousin Gerhard, Uncle Otto, my sister Helga, Cousin Kurt. (Picture Below) Mother is standing to my right.

(Picture below) Our little family. Mother, Helga and I are posing for Aunt Gretchen. Mother looks a little odd, because she had just been stung by a bee!

I am wearing a very pretty blue velvet dress made for me by a dressmaker in Tapiau. Mother later had this dress altered for my sister, Helga.

1941

My confirmation took place on April 6, 1941. This was a very special day for me because the entire family was able to attend this event. Large family gatherings were not always possible with the war going on.

The Urban family kindly arranged for a *Kutsche,* which was a small carriage drawn by two horses and this carriage enabled us to drive to the church in *Tapiau* as a family unit. Since we did not possess a car, this was a very special luxury for us and added to the festivity of the day.

My mother presented me with a Swiss wristwatch which had been ordered through the sister of my mother's employer. I looked at the watch and could hardly believe I was the owner of this treasure. What a lovely surprise for me! You see, watches in those days were not mass-produced, inexpensive and therefore commonplace and ultimately disposable as they are today. Instead, they were specially crafted by a skilled watchmaker and meant to be keepsakes.

Today, watches are only meant to last until the battery has to be changed and batteries are often more expensive than the watch. In those days, a watch was an heirloom you took good care of and then passed on to the next generation.

I was quite aware that this watch represented a long time of planning scrimping and saving on Mother's part, as well as some clever manoeuvring. Making purchases was not a simple matter with the ration card system that now regulated and dominated the marketplace.

During the war years, purchasing required considerable ingenuity and was generally limited to what was readily available. And certainly, we did not have shopping centers and "Big-Box" stores.

Mother also presented me with a new pretty white dress to wear for my confirmation and I was so thrilled because I had never owned such a nice dress. Somehow Mother had found a way to have it made for me, even though she did not have a lot of money.

I remembered that my mother once bought several meters of cloth without a ration card. Instead of using her ration card, she had traded our own smoked meat and eggs for the cloth. People who lived in the country were fortunate that way; we had more opportunities for trading.

I was so happy that day, for reaching this important milestone in my life, for my two wonderful presents and because most of the family could be together to celebrate the day with me — even my relatives from *Königsberg* were there.

Although the occasion for this family get-together was my confirmation, I think we were also celebrating the fact that our family unit was still intact. With the war upsetting the simple life we had known until then, everyone was probably very aware that this might be the last time for quite a while, where we could all share each other's company.

Unfortunately Grandfather did not live to see this day. I still missed him terribly and thought about the words of wisdom he would have offered.

My Uncle Albert, Mother's younger brother, was already in the army and I hadn't expected him to come. I did not know that he had arranged for a special leave of absence and that Aunt Frieda had wanted to surprise me.

She had contrived for my absence and then asked Uncle Albert to hide in the pantry until she gave him the signal to present himself. At that opportune moment, when he jumped out to embrace me, I almost burst into tears.

Perhaps I was a little nervous in spite of my happiness, because I knew that Uncle Karl, Mother's older brother, would be drafted soon. In the midst of my special day, a dark cloud hung over our little house in *Imten.*

My mind was suddenly in turmoil, distressed with thoughts of the future. What purpose could this war possibly bring? When would the war end? Will my uncles come home safely? When could we go back to the way we were?

My confirmation was an important milestone in my life. I was very proud of this white dress and new Swiss watch. I was also very proud of Mother's clever manoeuvring.

It was my special day and yet a dark cloud hung over our little house in Imten. How would this war change our lives? Would my uncles return home safely?

MY FIRST JOBS

In 1941, I completed my schooling and in April of that year I started to work in earnest. Up until this time, Grandmother had kept me occupied with domestic chores at home. Now it was time to earn actual wages and to contribute to the family in a financial way as well and I was looking forward to my introduction to the adult world.

My first job was to keep house for the Böhnke family in *Tapiau*, who were relatives of the Böhnkes in *Imten*. This was a difficult job for a fifteen-year-old girl because I was responsible for taking care of two little children, cleaning the house, doing the washing by hand, and preparing all the meals. This is quite a job, when you don't have the modern conveniences we have today. I was a little overwhelmed, to say the least.

Mr. and Mrs. Böhnke left every morning for work and expected lunch to be ready precisely when they returned at noon. Sometimes I would frantically refer to a cook book as I did not have all that much experience cooking different types of meals. By comparison, our meals at home had always been very plain — mainly milk soups, boiled fish, potatoes and cabbage. Even though we had our own sausages, we did not eat meat every day. It was obvious to me that the Böhnkes expected more than the simple fare I was used to eating.

I worked there from April 1941 to April 1942 and earned sixty DM per month, but this job was a lot to handle for a young girl. One day Mother came to the house, took a look around and suddenly declared:

"You are not staying here!"

She explained that I was too young to be doing the work of an adult. And that was that!

Mother could be very strong-willed and had no fear of authority if she perceived injustice, however minor. In this case, Mother felt that the Böhnkes were taking advantage of my inexperience and believed that she needed to take control of the situation.

Perhaps because she had always had to fend for herself and knew that there was no gentleman who would come to her rescue, she knew how to take life by the horns. That is how she lived her life. She probably expected the same fortitude from me, but somehow she must have known that I was not quite ready yet.

Mother quickly made some enquiries and a few weeks later, I was able to start work for a dairy cooperative as a house-maid. This was also quite a large household, but my employers had another maid as well. This maid took care of all the cooking and baking and other domestic chores.

There were four young children and my main job was to care for them. I worked there from May 1942 to August 1944 and earned eighty DM per month and enjoyed this position very much. As was customary in those days, this money was given to Mother, who used it to support our family.

Taking care of children was intended to be just my first job, because Mother had plans for me to eventually learn the seamstress trade. In the meantime, she would make arrangements for an apprenticeship in *Tapiau*. She considered the seamstress trade to be an opportunity for me to establish my independence. In her opinion, this trade promised a better future than working as a house-maid or farm-hand. But the war would change all our plans.

1944

By July 1944, the war had invaded every part of our daily lives and we could hear the almost constant sound of artillery in the distance. The engines of war seemed to be coming closer all the time.

Every day brought horrific news and long lists of soldiers who had died in combat. The peaceful life I had known in *Imten* seemed like a dream now.

Surely the war would end one day? But what would the end of the war mean to us? East Prussia was already cut off from the rest of Germany. Would we be severed even more? These dark thoughts tormented us and made it impossible to live normally.

Towards the end of 1944, huge numbers of refugee families started to come into our region. They were fleeing from the approaching Russian army and clutching with desperate resignation to what remained of their lives. I watched in anxiety, as long columns of refugees from farther east passed through our area.

Their horses dragged small wagons packed with their most precious possessions. Some would stop in our village for a rest. It was heartbreaking to look into their eyes; to acknowledge the terrible truth that no one wanted to speak out loud. Where is this war leading us? What would happen to us now?

These weary families would ask if they could use our stove so that they could prepare something to eat; perhaps a goose or a chicken that they had brought with them. Most of the time, they would sleep on their wagons and move on the next morning.

We watched them sadly and wondered if they would arrive safely at their destinations. We prayed for them and tormented ourselves with questions that had no answers. *Will we be next? Must we leave our homeland too?*

It is difficult to imagine today. How can you leave a home where your family has lived for generations? How can you abandon farms and huge estates that had passed down from one generation to the next? Everything had always been so orderly in our lives. Our lives had always been so predictable. There is comfort in predictability.

This comfortable predictability, this cherished security would soon be gone forever. Now no one knew where to go, or if it would ever be possible to return again. The First World War had been so different. Who could imagine the total collapse of this beautiful region? Who could believe that East Prussia would become a victim of "ethnic cleansing"? Who could foresee that our cultural heritage would be lost forever?

What do you take with you when you are forced to leave your home so abruptly? What do you leave behind? An order to evacuate would come eventually, we all knew that. Pack your belongings. You have two hours to leave your home. That's what officials would say to us when it was our turn to go. It was just a matter of time.

When the time came, everyone faced the same dilemma, whether you were an ordinary farm hand or estate owner. How do you pack your life into a wagon? Only the essentials, we would be told. What is essential to your life? Often, cows, pigs and chickens had to stay behind. What would become of them?

In October, I was still working and living in *Tapiau* but in the first week of December as the crisis heightened, officials sent me to work in *Königsberg*. There, I was drafted into the *Kriegshilfdienst*, an auxiliary civilian service. The intention was optimistic, this group would assist civilians displaced by the war. But as young as I was, I knew *Königsberg* was lost. It was too late.

In *Königsberg*, social agencies and infrastructure were collapsing all around me. I was seventeen years old, witnessing a wild frenzy of destruction and the death of a beautiful city I had loved. I had spent so many summers here with my aunts. I no longer recognized the *Königsberg* that I once knew. And now, among desperate strangers trying to survive, trying to escape, I had no means of communicating with my family.

I had no idea of what faced them in the late autumn of 1944 and winter 1945 and I would only learn of Mother's flight from *Imten* many years later when we were reunited. I am reconstructing her story here from what

Grandmother, Aunt Hanna and Mother were able to tell me.

MOTHER'S FLIGHT

The time had come. What they had feared and anticipated was now reality. Mother knew what the Russian soldiers were capable of. She had heard enough horrific descriptions from the fleeing East Prussian refugees and this was more than she needed to make up her mind.

There was no time to lose; she had to take charge of the situation in order to save her family. Uncle Otto had been drafted too, so he was not there to help them escape the advancing Russian army.

Farmer Urban had left with his children and housekeeper months before, when the weather was still favourable. His wife had passed away some years earlier, and she was spared the destruction of their estate and the devastation that was to come.

Mother immediately negotiated for a wagon and a horse from the Urban Estate. Farmer Urban had taken several horses and the best horses had of course already been requisitioned. Never mind, Mother had thought stubbornly. She would make do with the horse Farmer Urban had left. She would always find a way. No matter what obstacles stood in front of her. Mother always knew what must be done.

But Grandmother did not want to leave Imten. Stubborn as always, Grandmother declared that she wanted to be buried beside her husband. The cemetery plot had been arranged for a long time ago and she would not abandon Grandfather's grave. Grandmother belonged to East Prussia and East Prussia belonged to her. How could it be otherwise?

"I'm not going! In the last war, we had to evacuate too. But just for a while. We were allowed to come back home. We'll be allowed to come back home this time too! You'll see!"

"It's different this time," replied Mother brusquely, as she surveyed the kitchen. What should she take along on this winter journey to a destination that was not yet clearly defined?

What would fit on the little wagon? Food from the pantry, some pots, plates, spoons, a few blankets, towels, socks, Aunt Gretchen's photographs. Grandfather's watch.

It was lucky for all of them that Mother was able to take charge. She would soon be forced to prove that she could be stronger and more stubborn than Grandmother. But she must not cry; she must conceal her fear, she told herself.

Aunt Hanna was not able to help her all that much. Mother reminded herself that she was always more practical than Aunt Hanna in any case, and besides, there was no time for criticism or sentimentality now.

It was time to make a decision and though Grandmother had always been the matriarch, from that moment on, Mother would make the decisions for the whole family. She had to.

"We cannot wait any longer, Mother! We must leave! Now! Before it's too late!"

Grandmother did not say anything this time. She watched Mother packing but refused to budge. It did not take Mother long to load the wagon.

Mother now looked at Grandmother; this woman who had always been a pillar of strength. Grandmother, who had always been consulted on any family matter. What could Mother do? She could not leave Grandmother behind! Mother had no alternative but to forcefully mount Grandmother on the wagon.

She placed Grandmother gently beside Aunt Hanna, who tried to calm her down. Helga, Fritz and Kurt watched in silence. They perceived the seriousness of their situation at once and realized that they had to listen to Mother. Even though Grandmother had always made decisions concerning the welfare of the family, Mother was in charge now. How painful it must have been for Mother, to have to treat her own mother like a child so that they could flee from the Russians.

There were no men around to help Mother, so the reins were quite literally in her hands. Mother was now responsible for caring and feeding her family and keeping them from freezing to death in the frigid temperature. Getting them to safety, although she did not have a clear idea of what this safety was or where it would lead them.

How far would they have to travel to escape the Russians? Where would she find enough food for the children when their food packages ran out? How would she find enough food for the horse in the middle of winter?

Mother looked at the poor horse that would have to travel that long stretch towards the coast. Was it strong enough to make this journey? This was an exceptionally cold January. And her horse wasn't even equipped with proper shoes.

They would have to travel for days in freezing temperatures. Mother rationed out the food carefully to make it last as long as possible. She always took the smallest portion and sometimes didn't eat anything for a whole day, pretending that she wasn't hungry. The children are growing. They need the nourishment more than I do, she said to herself.

Whenever they stopped to rest the horse, Mother would look for twigs and small branches. Pushing back the snow with her hands, she would set her makeshift kindling down to make a little fire. Taking a pot from the wagon, she would fill it with snow and let it melt on the fire, so that they could have drinking water.

The poor horse troubled Mother, but she did the best she could by gathering extra grass in the surrounding wooded areas. Warming it with her hands first, she would feed it slowly to the horse. Mother knew this was not enough for a horse travelling in winter, but what could she do?

How had they managed without a map? They were never alone; it seemed to Mother that all of East Prussia was moving towards the Frische Haff[8] to escape the Russians. As far as their eyes could see there were endless columns of wagons and weary travellers on foot. There were exhausted horses everywhere, moving very slowly, their heads hung down low.

Finally, they reached the coast. Imten and Königsberg were far behind them now. The shoreline was crowded with fleeing refugees and hysterical horses. Instinctively, the horses knew the danger of crossing ice.

"How will we ever cross that ice? Look! It's breaking apart everywhere," cried Fritz, my cousin.

Mother was silent. She knew there was no turning back now. Somehow, they must cross that stretch of treacherous ice. This was their only route to safety. There was no other choice for them. To stay behind or to return to Imten meant certain death at the hands of the Russian soldiers.

She trudged forward with strong determination, coaxing the horse, keeping the family intact. Trying to keep the horse calm, she spoke softly, soothingly. Keeping her eye on the distant shore, she bit her lip and refused to look back.

Mother examined the ice again. She would have to cross a thin sheet of ice, made all the more hazardous by the almost constant enemy bombing. It was a miracle that anyone could still cross. Mother observed closely and saw that some East Prussians were able to cross while others crashed through the ice. She prayed fiercely for another miracle so that her family could also survive this horror.

The ice was much too thin to carry the weight of the fleeing refugees, but the desperate East Prussians would not give up. Many left many of their priceless belongings on the shore, hoping that this sacrifice would be enough to get them across the ice.

The frantic screams of people breaking through the ice pierced her ears. All around her people and horses were drowning in the freezing water. And still the bombing would not stop. The eerie sound of machine guns came from somewhere, everywhere.

"Don't look, children, keep walking. Don't stop!" Mother kept walking, steadily, slowly, keeping an eye on Grandmother and watching out for Aunt Hanna, who was never very strong. There were hundreds of senseless deaths that day alone. Mother would learn only later that the death toll for fleeing East Prussians would be in the thousands.

"Be careful, be careful, children, please!" Mother blocked out the sound of screaming horses. She focused on her own horse.

"Just keep going, slowly slowly, careful now," she whispered to her horse. The rest of the family walked single file behind.

"We're almost there! Please, God, let us make it to the other side!" Mother closed her eyes and prayed.

When she opened her eyes again she realized that they had reached the other side. She counted everyone to make sure that all family members were still with her. Grandmother, Aunt Hanna, Fritz, Kurt and little

Helga. Yes, they were all there! They had made it! In spite of all the dangers of that day, Mother had managed to manoeuvre her horse around the broken ice, and succeeded in bringing the family across the "Frische Haff." They were alive! They were safe, for now!

Mother had been brought up with Christian faith and Prussian spirit and this helped her through the years. Their struggles were not yet over and her faith would be tested again and again in the years to come.

But she would never blame God for the tragedy and suffering of that cold winter in 1945. She just quietly thanked God that they had been able to escape from the Russian army in time, and prayed for the poor souls who were not able to. Her East Prussian spirit kept her going in face of danger and adversity yet to come.

Mother was not a woman who talked a lot or reflected on the whys and wherefores. Instead, she found and renewed her strength in hard work and caring for her family.

The distance from the *Frische Haff (Vistula Lagoon)* to the *Frische Nehrung* (Vistula Spit) looks so small on a map. But the distance from the lagoon to the Vistula Spit (the narrow peninsula that separates the lagoon from *Danzig Bay* or *Bay of Gdańsk*) varies from ten to thirty kilometres, depending on the crossing point. Since *Elbing* had fallen to the Russians on January 23, 1945, escape by land was impossible. There was no other choice for thousands of fleeing East Prussians but to cross the frozen lagoon. Crossing the ice was treacherous and enemy bombs wreaked havoc everywhere.

My mother was a courageous, hardworking and very independent woman. She kept her family alive in that fierce winter of 1945, when all the odds were against her.

AUXILIARY CIVILIAN SERVICE

My normal employment ended in October of 1944 and plans for my future apprenticeship were postponed indefinitely. This war had appropriated Mother's hopes for my future. Her dream that I would become a seamstress one day would never be realized. I understood this.

But how could I ever imagine that an immeasurable tragedy of human suffering would soon consume East Prussia? Or that I would witness horrors surpassing my worst nightmares?

I was now drafted into the *Kriegshilfdienst,* an auxiliary civilian service. I was too far away from my family to be of any help to them, and in any case, contact was impossible, since I did not have any means of communication at my disposal. From now on, I no longer had Grandmother or Mother to guide me.

As part of this auxiliary civilian service, I was obliged to assist in a variety of posts, due to the severe labour shortages almost everywhere. Wherever I turned, there was a sense of hopelessness in the air and a feeling that the world was coming to an end. But I had little time to think as I was jostled and pushed from one job to another.

At the tender age of seventeen, I was required to work "wherever help was needed". This was a very tall order in desperate times.

By November, the situation for East Prussia was painfully tragic. Help was needed everywhere and most people recognized the futility of our position. We were pushed to the breaking point and for many people it must have seemed like Armageddon.

In December 1944, I was sent to *Königsberg,* where I worked for the railway as a clerk. My brief career as a railway clerk came to a very abrupt end on January 23, 1945 because that same day evacuation orders came to leave *Königsberg.* In the chaos of that time, this meant I was virtually on my own. *Where do I go now? How will I ever manage?* This was all I could think of on that day.

I had been trained to handle emergencies, but no amount of training could have prepared me for what was to come. I had heard so many horror stories about what Russian soldiers did with German women and I was very frightened. For the first time in my life, I was entirely on my own. Who could I ask for help? My world was collapsing around me and I had no idea where my family was. I did not really know what my next move would be.

To go back to *Imten* was impossible, since all routes were cut off. How would I ever find my family now that our old reliable infrastructure was in shambles? *Where is my family? What can I do? How will I escape the advancing Russian army?*

PILLAU

I realized that I hadn't eaten for several hours, but this seemed a trivial concern somehow on January 23, 1945. At first, I remained with the other girls from the auxiliary *Kriegshilfdienst* group and we still tried our best to fulfil our duties even though evacuation orders had been given. We had been trained to assist in emergency situations, but this "emergency" was now beyond any human capacity to help, beyond hope.

There was a chilling devastation, despair and confusion everywhere we looked. We tried to stay together for a while, but the city was overcrowded with people all trying to flee from the advancing Russians. The situation was out of control.

Not really knowing where to go, what to do, I attached myself to another group of people who were trying to reach Pillau[9] situated approximately sixty kilometres from *König*sberg. I knew that *Pillau* was a port from where ships departed daily with refugees from East Prussia, so I thought this might be the best solution for me under the circumstances. I would learn later that almost half a million refugees passed through *Pillau* to escape to western and central Germany.

I marched forward with this group, wondering what the future had in store for us. *What will we find in Pillau? Where would we find a safe haven?*

I don't know how long we walked; I think that the trek from *Königsberg* to *Pillau* took us about three days. I don't know what we lived on. I think we were all so afraid, that we did not think of food. We just kept trudging west, following the sun to *Pillau*, as if that city would be our refuge, away from the misery we had seen in *Königsberg*. *Our troubles will be over then. Someone will help us.* So we thought.

But when we reached *Pillau* we were met with bleak anguish and distressing mass confusion and I realized that I would not find refuge there. I had to find a ship that would take me to away from here, but since so many people were fleeing at the same time, the ships were hopelessly overloaded.

Everyone was pushing to get onto the ships. Women with children and old people were to be let on first, others had to wait. But from what I could see, we were mostly women, children and old people.

Eventually, I found a ship that was still accepting "passengers" and I found myself crammed together with several thousand women, children and old people. Unfortunately, in the turmoil, I did not take note of the name of the vessel and the exact day of departure. The shock of leaving *Königsberg* and the surreal days that followed had robbed my sense of time.

All I know for sure is that I am thankful it was not the *General von Steuben*. The *General von Steuben* left *Pillau*, heading for *Kiel* on February 9, 1945, packed with refugees and wounded soldiers. On February 10, 1945 it was torpedoed by the Russians and sank with about 4,300 passengers. I would learn this only much later.

GOTENHAFEN

So many of the refugees on those ships would not reach their destination. Much later, we would hear reports that Russian and American bombs were responsible for sinking the *Wilhelm Gustloff*, *General von Steuben*, *Goya* and *Cap Arcona*.

The sinking of these four ships alone resulted in the deaths of about twenty thousand people who were merely fleeing for their lives. This figure attributed to wasted human lives is incomprehensible to me. The only way I can imagine the impact of these twenty thousand deaths, is to visualize about sixty little towns the size of *Imten* all destroyed at once.

But my life would be spared. By a strange twist of fate, by the mere coincidence of timing, I did not get on one of those ships that sank in the cold Baltic Sea.

The ship that would bring me to *Gotenhafen* was so full that there was almost no room for anyone to sit. It was very uncomfortable to stand for such a long period of time.

Some people carried little bundles and these served as a bed or place to rest. For others, who had suffered so much, who had lost their families, or whose children had not survived the cold trek to *Pillau*, the discomforts and lack of food hardly mattered any more. They were numb from the shock of civilization disintegrating around them. Others prayed desperately, hoping that their voices would be heard amid the bombs flying from the sky.

How do you stay clean in these circumstances? I had always been meticulously neat and fastidious about cleanliness. That too, was far from my mind now. When was the last time I could wash myself since leaving *Königsberg?* Proper hygiene became a minor issue now. In any case, no one had access to the handy disinfectant kits or soap dispensers that would be available today.

Survival was my first concern, and I silently prayed that our ship would not be bombed by the Russians. *Please let us live! Let us return to our families! We are civilians. What do we have to do with this war?* Today, I realize how very lucky we all were on that ship. My prayers were answered when our ship eventually arrived in *Gotenhafen.*

COLLECTION AREA

In *Gotenhafen,* we were told to proceed to a collection area. Again there were so many people! We were supposed to wait in a collection area so that we could be transported by rail to the western regions of Germany.

Finding railway transportation was no easy task, because so many tracks had been bombed by the allies. Had they done this on purpose? It seemed so deliberate to us. As if they did not want East Prussian refugees to make it to safety.

I ended up staying at this camp in *Gotenhafen* for about ten days and met an elderly lady who was kind enough to share some of the little food she had. She offered to take me to her daughter who was already in the western part of Germany and I had almost made up my mind to go with her.

My options were so limited, and I was clutching at a small straw, clinging to a stranger, just hoping for survival. I often wonder today, how my life would have turned out, had I accepted her offer.

Perhaps fate had something else in store for me, because everything took a turn in the midst of all this turmoil, when by the craziest of coincidences, I saw my cousin Irene, my Aunt Frieda's daughter. Here, now, at this wretched site. I could hardly believe my eyes and was so thrilled to see a member of my family at this crowded camp!

I was aware that people who were able to make private arrangements for accommodation would be permitted to leave the camp, so I explained my position to the camp personnel and chose to leave. I believed that I would be better off with my own relatives.

PASSAGE TO BUBLITZ

Irene said that I should go with her, so I followed her and met up with my Aunt Frieda, who was part of a group with two other women and their children. Together they had sought refuge in the abandoned house where I now found myself. I was so grateful to be among family again.

I learned that Aunt Frieda had left her home in *Zopen* in the hope that she would somehow be able to make it to her sister's house in *Bottrop*[10]. My Aunt Frieda and her two children, Irene and Gerhard had lived just a few kilometres from our house back in *Imten* and now we were here, sharing a house that other refuges had left behind. I was so happy that this part of my family was still alive. To find them here was truly a miracle.

We stayed in this deserted house for a couple of days and then tried again to obtain transportation. Finally we got passage to *Bublitz*[11]. Together, we left for *Bublitz* — Mrs. König, Mrs. Mass, her two children, my Aunt Frieda, Irene and Gerhard.

Unfortunately, we would find out that it was not possible to go any further than *Bublitz*. Such a short distance had taken us days, but at least we were still together, and I was so thankful for that small blessing.

Exhausted, we got off the train, and walked for a while, and soon we encountered an old farmer. With a weary and forlorn-looking expression, he advised us to keep walking towards *Drawenen.*

"I have seen such terrible things, you should not stay in *Bublitz*", he said in despair.

"But we are so tired! And we have been travelling for days," I explained.

He pleaded with us again and again.

"Please don't stay here! You cannot stay here; it would be much too dangerous for you!"

It took us about two hours to walk to *Drawenen*. While walking, we quietly prayed that we would find safety there. And a place to sleep. And food. What we had salvaged from the house in *Gotenhafen* was already gone. We were hungry.

DRAWENEN

On February 18, 1945 we arrived in *Drawenen*. There, we were taken care of by a farming family who treated us very well and fed us. Our good fortune would last just a few days, because soon the Russian soldiers would hunt us down here as well.

Hearing of these new troubles in this area, the farmer in *Drawenen* said that we should hide ourselves in the large haystack on his property. He was just trying to protect us, because he was aware of the constant threat of rape by Russian soldiers.

For whatever reason, we chose not to follow his advice. This decision saved our lives, because Russians strafed the area all night. We would not have survived in the haystack.

The farmer had two Polish farm hands, one of whom would save our lives from a Russian soldier a few days later. The first Russian soldiers who arrived in *Drawenen* did not harm us, although they took away what few possessions we still had.

In my case, I would have to forfeit my wristwatch. The lovely Swiss watch that Mother had given me for my confirmation would only be a memory from that day on.

I was very sad about losing my wristwatch, but I could not cry when I thought about what other East Prussians had lost. Still, the Russian soldier's justification seemed insanely illogical to me.

"If I don't take your watch, the next soldiers that pass through surely will, so you may as well give it to me," he had said.

What difference would it make to me, if all Russian soldiers were thieves? Did he really think *that* realization would alleviate my sorrow? Did he imagine that he deserved my watch more than the other Russian soldiers?

I was heartbroken about the loss of my watch, because I knew how difficult it had been for Mother to obtain it. I wondered how that Russian soldier would later justify his actions to his friends and relatives. Or to himself. Would he not be ashamed to admit exactly how he had come to possess such a fine watch? Perhaps one day, when he looked over his life, he would think about this. How could he be proud of robbing a young girl?

The next group of Russian soldiers that passed through left us alone, but this relative calm would not last long. The next morning, the horror would start all over again when a mounted Russian soldier approached the house.

He got off his horse, entered our quarters, took a look around and then quickly grabbed me by the arm. Shouting in Russian, he pulled me toward the farmer's bedroom. I turned white with fear. Aunt Frieda and the rest of the group could only watch in terror.

He placed his gun on the night table. I begged and cried, trying to make him understand that I was a young girl still — only seventeen years old and still a virgin. I was so scared. He was such an ugly man, with cruel slanted eyes and a pock-marked face.

But of course my crying did not help me. My fate was no different than that of possibly hundreds of thousands of other women in those terrifying days. I know that now. All I can say is that I was raped; violated in the most frightening manner a young woman of that time could only imagine. But those three words cannot describe the horror and revulsion I felt.

Today, I still wonder what causes such monstrous behaviour. How would such men feel if their own grandmothers, mothers, aunts, and children had been treated as we were treated? What satisfaction can there be to rape a defenceless, innocent girl? I do not have the answer. Not even today and I am eighty years old now.

The terror went on for several days. There were two other girls there, and the same thing happened to them. Over and over again. We felt numb, and so very forlorn and abandoned.

One evening, a Russian officer who looked about thirty years old, took me to a room in the farm house and motioned for me to lie down with him. Again, I braced myself, fearing the worst.

I cried, knowing that my tears were useless. To my surprise, he did not touch me. But outside I could hear the banging against the door. Other soldiers were shouting and trying to get in. This officer beside me shouted back and then all was still.

Perhaps he had some authority over the drunken mob outside. Perhaps he had a daughter of his own back in Russia. Perhaps he was able to feel pity for young girls trapped here, away from their mothers and fathers.

Perhaps he was only different from all the other Russian soldiers who had passed through.

I will never know why this Russian officer acted the way he did, but he left me alone that night and actually let me go back to my Aunt Frieda. She, together with the other women, had prepared their bedding on the floor of the farm house. In my exhaustion, I quickly lay down beside my aunt. I only wanted to sleep. And to forget. And to erase all the horror of the last few days. But we would not be able to get sleep that night.

More Russians soldiers had arrived. A wild, drunken group. They were shrieking and firing their guns into the air, as if there were no end to their ammunition. I was so afraid that they would break down the door and kill us all. Then, finally the shooting stopped.

One of them came barging into our little refuge and ordered us to get out and stand in front of the house. Terrified, we all did as we were told — Mrs. Mass, Mrs. König, the children, Aunt Frieda, cousin Gerhard and cousin Irene and I moved silently towards the front of the house. What would they do with us now?

We said our prayers and expected to die right there. This soldier was very drunk and threatened us constantly with his rifle. In broken German, he shouted that German soldiers had killed his brother and now he would kill us.

"You deserve to die!" he said, crazed with his thirst for revenge.

The Polish farmhand, whom I mentioned earlier, heard the commotion and intervened.

"Leave those women alone, they are not to blame for the war," he pleaded.

He was able to speak Russian and somehow able to convince the Russian soldier that we were innocent of any wrong doing.

"They are simply young farm girls trapped, fleeing from the war, like so many other refugees right now," he continued.

To our amazement, the Russian soldier decided not to shoot us after all. This Polish farm hand saved our lives that day. The drunken soldiers moved on and we had a little reprieve.

We realized that this farm hand had risked his own life to save our lives, for who can predict the actions of a drunken crowd of men? Once more, I had miraculously escaped death. I did not take this for granted and whispered a prayer of thanks.

Our misery would last another fourteen days. Russians soldiers would pass through again and again. Their monstrous behaviour would repeat itself over and over, but at least no one threatened to shoot us anymore.

Though sometimes we thought *that* would be a more merciful end to our despair. When would this bestial cruelty end?

On March 6, 1945 three Russian soldiers came to our quarters looking for girls. Since our arrival, other women had sought refuge with us. There were so many of us now, and we were easy targets. What did these soldiers want with us? What was different?

These women had left other places of "refuge" because they believed it would be safer with us. Indeed, the farm house was a little distance from the main road and not quite so visible.

All of these women had experienced the savagery of Russian soldiers and did not know where else to turn. Where do you go when there is no place to run to anymore? Are you better off with a group? Are you better off on your own? We did not know.

So we huddled together, in the mistaken assumption that there is safety in numbers. What is left to do, except to hope for the best? To hope that somehow you will survive, in spite of everything. Even if it is only until the next day.

The three soldiers selected three young girls from our group and I was among them. Singled out that way, I felt doomed. *What was in store for me now?* One of the soldiers explained that we were needed to work for a couple of weeks, but after what we had been through, how could we believe them?

In tears, the farmer's wife gave each of us a portion of bread and a small piece of ham. We said our goodbyes to all the women who had become close friends during our stay together. I worried for them and I wondered if I would ever see my Aunt Frieda or cousins again. We left with the three soldiers. *Where will they take us? Will we be violated again?*

BACK TO BUBLITZ

While we were marching back towards *Bublitz,* more and more young girls and women joined our group. Russian soldiers guarded us constantly. When we finally arrived back in *Bublitz,* we realized that there are now about a hundred of us.

In the distance we were able to see a huge fire and in our fear, we thought that the Russians are going to burn us alive. This was no wild imagination on our part, because we had all witnessed the unspeakable cruelties some Russian soldiers were capable of.

In all these weeks of marching, we had seen how each farm house had a tale to tell. There was sad evidence of brutality and cruelty everywhere.

But we were directed away from the raging fire. Instead, we were brought to a large building, possibly a hotel in better times. There were several hundreds of people crowded on the floor of the cellar of this building and the Russian soldiers informed us that we would have to stay here.

We ended up staying several days. There was very little to eat, because the Russians believed that most people had brought some food with them. But the little we had among us was already gone. The bit of ham and bread I had been given by the farmer's wife, I had already shared with people who had nothing.

INTERROGATIONS

Each morning, a group of girls was led to a room upstairs, where they were interrogated by Russian officers who were accompanied by interpreters. Eventually we would all get a turn at being asked whether our parents were in the "party" and what our families owned in property or goods and many other questions which seemed like nonsense to us.

Why did they ask such silly questions, we wondered. Most of us came from simple farm families who had no time for or interest in politics. We were too busy working, tending our animals and keeping our farms going. Especially since 1939, when everything was so scarce, and work was doubly hard. What did all this foolishness signify?

By the middle of March 1945, the interrogations appeared to be over. Each person in this group had been interrogated at least once. Soon, we would again have to leave what had become familiar surroundings. Again, we would have to tread into the unknown.

We were herded towards a church and ended up staying there several days. We had nothing to do here but to wait and worry about what they would do with us. It was a little more comfortable in this church, where we could at least sit in the pews and rest our legs a little. Guarded constantly by Russian soldiers with bayonets, we were still very fearful that they were going to rape us, but we were left alone this time.

Our stay in this church was only brief. Would there be no end to this marching? Where would be our destination this time?

A few days later, we found ourselves at a railway station. Here, we were ordered to get into the nearby cattle cars. How long would we stay in this new prison, I wondered.

TOILETS

Every couple of hours, a Russian guard armed with a bayonet, came to take us to a "toilet". He marched with us to the back of the yard where a gigantic hole had been dug to serve as a latrine of sorts.

Beams had been placed across the hole for us to sit on. There was no privacy for us and we all wondered what right the Russians had to degrade us in this way. *Did our welfare not matter to anyone? Where was the Red Cross?*

This "toilet area" was surrounded by a large barbed-wire fence and the male and female Russian soldiers sat nearby and shouted at us.

"Look at you, you filthy German pigs."

We looked straight ahead and pretended not to notice them.

This cattle-car prison was actually a depot from which groups of women were transported to other centres, we would learn. A few days later, we were called to the yard so that we could be counted. This was a procedure that would be repeated over and over again throughout my time in Russia. How bizarre to count us so often, when we didn't seem to matter to anyone, I thought.

There was a grim purpose to the counting after all. The guards warned us over and over again that for every escapee, ten prisoners would be shot. I don't believe anyone in my group thought of escape. Where could we escape to?

We were trapped in this cattle-car for four days and we were so hungry. Some girls had a plate and spoon with them and tried desperately to demonstrate that we were hungry.

Repeatedly, we used a variety of sign language techniques to communicate to the Russian soldiers that we were very hungry and thirsty. Surely these Russians could not be so cruel — to let us starve, or die of thirst, trapped here in these cattle cars?

A few minutes later, a Russian guard snarled at us and threw a large piece of raw meat into our cattle car. A woman who could understand Russian translated his words for us: "Here's some food, you German pigs! Eat!"

FROM BUBLITZ TO KONITZ

The next morning, we were roused from our cattle-car prison. Guards counted us again and divided us into groups. *What was in store for us now? Where are we going?*

All we knew is that we had to march. Just put one foot in front of the other and keep moving. That first day, we were forced to march approximately thirty kilometres and the next day we would march for another thirty kilometres. Where were we going now? We were so tired, thirsty and hungry that we could barely walk.

We were permitted to rest for fifteen minutes, twice a day, during this long march, but thirst was always a problem. If we were lucky to find a stream along the way, we would rush to swallow a few quick mouthfuls of water, cupping the water carefully in our hands.

Sometimes a decomposing horse lay beside the stream, but we did not care anymore. We were so thirsty that nothing mattered but getting a drink of water to quench our parched throats. If we were lucky enough to see a water pump in a village that we marched through, sometimes the Russian guards would let us stop to get a drink of water.

But this is easier said than done when crowds of people charge at the same time towards a single water pump. In any case, one person would have to work the pump. So it was not always possible for everyone to get a drink in the short time that was given us.

At least we were fed every evening. Each prisoner received one small piece of boiled beef and two little potatoes. We guessed that most likely the source for our evening meal was a dead cow — one of many that lay strewn on the roads everywhere we marched. Cows, too, were victims of this war.

NINETY KILOMETRES

Outbreaks of diarrhoea and dysentery were common by this time, which was not a surprise because we were drinking mostly contaminated water. Dysentery is an illness involving severe diarrhoea that is often associated with bloody stools. You don't hear much about this disease anymore; it is caused by ingestion of food or water containing bacteria.

In three days, we had marched approximately ninety kilometres. When we did not march quickly enough, the Russian guard jabbed us with their rifles. Prisoners at the end of a column always got the worst treatment. I always tried to walk as quickly as I could so that I could maintain a position in the middle of a column. It was a little safer there.

Time would never erase the images of what I witnessed during this long march. Right and left in the ditches, there were eerie vestiges of gruesome encounters or failed escape attempts. Corpses of East Prussians who had tried to flee from the oncoming Russian soldiers and not made it. Perhaps some of them had just frozen to death in the frigid Prussian winter.

Dead animals were everywhere. Starved dogs, huddled by abandoned wagons. Slashed suitcases and baskets torn apart. I assumed that the Russians had simply taken horses when they were still in relatively good condition, and left the wagons for other scavengers.

But I could also see how many poor horses had not been able to carry their load anymore, in their weakened condition. Obviously, this is the result when people are forced to flee in winter, and food is very scarce. Those poor horses, I thought. Uncle Otto was always so proud of the beautiful horses on the Urban Estate. It would break his heart to see this.

KONITZ

Had my family managed to escape? Or were they left for dead in a ditch somewhere between here and Pillau? What had become of all the other people trapped in East Prussia?

So many worries preoccupied me and oppressed me while I trudged on. I marched mechanically, trying desperately to suppress my feelings. Trying not to think.

At least the weather had been kind for the last few days. It had been an early spring and I had seen many pretty flowers along the march. The sun warmed us for a little while. Nature provided such beauty in the spring and yet the world had become so ugly for us.

I could not make sense of why this was happening to us. As far as I could determine, we were just women of various ages and simple country girls from East Prussia. I speculated about this over and over again, but I could not find any answers.

What did the Russians want with us? Why are we still here? The war was over, wasn't it? Or almost over. Why are we still here now against our will?

On the fourth day, we had arrived in *Schlochau*[12] and we were informed that we were required to march only another ten kilometres. This is a very long distance on an almost empty stomach.

On the fifth day, we arrived in *Konitz*. It was now March 18, 1945. Here, we were forced into a large prison, where we were divided up into small cells of five to six women per cell.

In this prison, we were also fed on a regular basis, but still just once a day, as before. A large bowl of soup, and dried bread was our daily fare.

The soup was made with barley and potatoes, so it was not too thin and offered some nourishment to hungry prisoners. It had even been prepared using bay leaves as flavouring and someone commented that perhaps the cook was a German prisoner! It seemed to have been made in the German style. But it was not served in the German style, I had thought cynically.

I was horrified to see that the bowls were not washed! Prisoners would get a full bowl, devour the soup quickly, and then Russian servers would simply refill the same bowl and pass it to the next hungry prisoner.

I closed my eyes and tried not to think about the dirty fingerprints on the outside of the bowl, or about how many other mouths had touched the same filthy bowl. I thought of Aunt Gerda's pristine china and her lovely white table cloth. How can these Russians treat us with so little dignity? We are not animals. But I was so hungry. So very hungry.

On March 26, we were informed that we were being prepared for a longer journey — we would be transported to Russia! In cattle cars, from what we could see! How far was it from *Konitz* to Russia? How would we survive such a long trip in cattle cars? Was our one meal of soup and dried bread with water per day supposed to sustain us for the long trip to Russia?

Our final destination would be *Ufa* we had learned, by gleaning bits of information from various sources. It was situated somewhere in the Ural Mountains, someone told me.

How far away was Ufa from Konitz? How many bowls of soup would we be fed until we reached Ufa?

The guards seemed to want to get rid of us as quickly as possible, and pushed and prodded us irritably as they herded us into the cattle cars. Sometimes, they shouted wildly and jabbed us with their rifles if we did not move quickly enough for their liking.

TRAIN TO UFA

I reflected that my departure to Russia would take place on March 26, 1945 — my eighteenth birthday! How I had looked forward to my eighteenth birthday! Back then, in *Ostpreussen*, I had often dreamed of the freedom I would have when I reached that magical age! How I would finally be able to go to the movies and stay out a little later at night. Curfews were so strict in those days!

Now I thought back to all that had happened to *Ostpreussen*, and all that had happened to me since January 23, 1945. That date would remain etched in my mind forever. As would this date. March 26, 1945! My departure from *Königsberg* seemed so long ago. So far away.

Now I was leaving for Russia — even farther away. *Where was my family? What had happened to my mother and grandmother and the rest of my family? Were they also taken prisoner by Russian soldiers? What had happened to Aunt Frieda, Irene and Gerhard? Are they also being transported to Russia?*

These railway cars were very uncomfortable since they were not equipped with seats. The best we could do was to lean against the side of the car or against each other.

This journey to *Ufa* would take about three weeks, but having so little to eat was not the worst part of our trip. There were no toilets on the train and we were not permitted to leave the rail car to relieve ourselves. This was a nightmare for all who experienced this miserable situation. *Barbaric. Inhumane. Cruel. These words are not adequate to describe how we are being treated. How will I ever survive this journey to Russia?*

The will to survive must be very strong. In such tight quarters, I soon became acquainted with the other women in my section and we tried to cheer each other up, holding on to our faith and belief that tomorrow would be better. *Nothing could possibly get worse than this.*

As wretched as we felt, we would not give up, we vowed. We would simply keep looking forward, thinking of the day that we could go home again. Every day we hoped and prayed that our situation would improve. Our faith gave us strength and there was some comfort in the fact that we were not alone in our deprivation and suffering.

Things will get better. Just beyond the horizon. Perhaps tomorrow. Or at the latest next month. Or when the rest of the world learned of these atrocities.

But deprivation and suffering are relative terms, we would learn. What is the difference between "worse" and "worst"? What yardstick is used to measure despair? How do you weigh misery?

Eventually, the Russian guards realized that we needed toilet facilities. A square opening of about twenty centimetres in diameter was roughly cut out on the floor of our rail car to serve as our "toilet" for the duration of the trip. This was their solution for the forty women that were imprisoned in each wagon.

For our three-week journey, we had no water for washing ourselves and the clothing on our backs was all we owned. It didn't matter here.

When was the last time I changed my clothing? When was the last time I washed my hands?

We felt best while the train was moving, and we tried to convince ourselves then that we felt warm. Actually, the farther east we travelled, the colder it was for us. It was not yet April and we were not dressed for the weather, and the cold made our hunger worse.

I was now with a group of five other young women. Their names were Renate, Eva, Inge, Waltraud and Ruth. We had stayed close together since *Bublitz*, and we supported each other as best we could. Every morning, we checked each other's hair for head lice. This was a very real concern in the confinement of our wagon. How do you keep your hair clean, when there is not enough drinking water, let alone soap and water to wash with?

During the day, sunlight flashed through the cracks and small holes in the train, and this dancing sunshine was a delight when there was so little else to cheer us. We had nothing with which to occupy our time, and so we tried to invent little games to keep our minds stimulated and to blot out the squalor.

What is your mother's recipe for potato pancakes? What are the ingredients for Goulash? Name all the meals you can think of that begin with "E".

But all the while, we were quite aware that we were being taken deeper into Russia. And we were very worried.

What is Russia like? What are the Russian people like? What will happen to us there?

I noticed that some women were slowly becoming hardened to all the insanity of this aftermath of the war. No one seemed to cry much anymore, it seemed. Although there were lots of reasons to cry.

Perhaps this was a kind of survival mechanism. An extraordinary method of conserving strength that may be needed later. When you have lost everything, you soon realize that it is no use to cry.

Crying will not bring back my mother, my father, my child. Crying will not warm my body. Crying will not give me something to eat.

At least there were no more occurrences of rape and we were all grateful that the Russian soldiers no longer molested us. At least I can maintain this for our group of forty women. I do not know for certain how it was for others on this train.

Often the train would stand still for hours. We would shiver in the wagon, huddling for warmth and we would be so happy when the train would start to move again. Small blessings in hard times.

Once we stopped at a larger station. The doors to our wagon were opened, but there was no chance that anyone would jump out because the Russian guards were always there. However, I was able to catch a glimpse of many other wagons carrying German men.

What does this mean? How many Germans are being taken to Russia? Will I see my relatives on another train bound for Russia?

In our wagon, there were three sisters and a sister-in-law who had managed to stay together all this time. After all the marching we had been through, this was quite remarkable. Suddenly, one of the sisters jumped up and cried out:

"Look! There's father!"

I looked to see where she had pointed and noticed a man of about sixty. We realized later that this wagon was actually joined to our train. I wondered if they would be united with their father when we reached our destination.

FIRST RUSSIAN CAMP

Our train stopped at an internment camp in a wooded area. After three weeks of travelling, we could finally disembark. The Russians had organized sleds that were to take us further into the woods. Quietly, we speculated amongst ourselves. *What will our new prison be like? Will we be fed regularly? Will we get more than one meal a day?*

I was very distressed to learn that the Russian guard wanted to separate me from my five friends. They had become very dear to me and I did not want to lose them now and have to go to *Ufa* alone. We pleaded with him and cried, but of course the guard was not moved by our little sorrows.

But someone had heard us, and explained that we would all end up in the same camp, so this separation would be only temporary. The man was Polish but could speak German as well as Russian. We were so relieved that we would not be separated. Here, in Russia, all we had was each other and we clung fiercely to our friendship.

NEW DEPRIVATIONS

Our journey by sled would last for several kilometres. This internment camp was ironically located in a beautiful wooded setting, but was severely marred by the barbed wire fence that surrounded it. There were guards stationed at all four corners of the camp.

We had been brought to a place built for the most evil criminals and yet we were mostly just girls and young women and a few elderly women. *How strange the world has become after the war. Now innocent people are imprisoned behind barbed wire. How can this be permitted?*

In front of me there were some mothers, who had been separated from their children by the Russian soldiers. There were also a few women over fifty years of age. There was an elderly lady, who must have been almost seventy years old, and she had her daughter with her.

It soon became obvious that we would be working here.

So we are to be considered as mere booty in this crazy war. What did all of this mean? What had we done to deserve this? Are there no international laws to prevent us from being used as slave labour? Did they expect elderly women to perform hard physical work as well?

In this camp, we would experience new deprivations. But at least they fed us first. That evening, we were given a bowl of soup and a piece of very heavy bread. After the meal, we were directed to a "washing" room. There we were instructed to wash ourselves.

We were horrified to learn that we were expected to put our heads in the same tub of water. Apparently some sort of chemical de-lousing agent had been added to the water. At least, that is what we were told.

Until that point, I did not have head-lice, because my friends and I had spent hours carefully examining each other's scalp for the last few weeks. But head-lice reproduce very quickly and the unsanitary conditions here aggravated the situation.

Women, who until now had been spared this added misery, would eventually get head-lice at this camp. One by one, we would have to submit to having our heads shaved, as a measure to control head lice. I watched sadly, as my hair fell to the ground. My once shiny dark blond strands that Grandmother had brushed and braided regularly were a handicap here. Later, typhoid fever would break out as well, compounding our troubles.

WORKING IN RUSSIA

To our surprise, we did not have to start working immediately, but were given a fourteen-day "vacation". We were fed a half-litre of thin soup daily and were given a half-litre of hot water to drink.

The soup consisted of some cabbage leaves, fish bones, and a cup of millet. It smelled terrible and I suspected that the fish was rancid. Again, there was a piece of bread to accompany our meal. The weight of this bread was supposed to be six hundred and fifty grams but it was so wet, that its nutritional value was questionable.

Some women looked at this meal and simply declared "I can't eat this garbage." Unfortunately, these women would soon die of starvation, because there was really nothing else to eat. The rest of us knew that we had to force this unappetizing gruel down our throats, so that we could get something into our stomachs for nourishment. So that we would survive. That was the only option we had.

Our sleeping quarters consisted of boards that had been nailed together, making long rows that stretched thirty to forty meters. There were three levels of these "sleeping boards" to accommodate a couple of hundred women and young girls. In the middle of the room there was a wooden plank to walk on.

After the fourteen days of "rest" were over, we were divided into work crews. Our duties consisted of felling large trees, cutting them into meter-long sections and sorting these into piles. The Russians showed us how to do this once and then we had to fend for ourselves. It was not easy work for malnourished women.

Women who had never done hard physical work before had a very difficult time adjusting to these conditions. Soon we would witness how one by one, the weaker women would get sick with typhoid fever. Some women would survive the typhoid fever, many others would not.

BURYING THE DEAD

Eventually, typhoid fever was rampant in every corner of the camp. We were horrified to see so many German prisoners dying off like flies. Every evening we could see six to ten women and men carried off to be disposed of.

Disposal was simple and final and there was no real recognition of their death. That a human being had lost the struggle to live under these horrendous conditions was of no significance here. No tears, No prayers. Just a final disposal. A sad end to human beings, who by a cruel twist of fate found themselves trapped in this cold, cold land.

Our camp was located in a small valley surrounded by little hills. During the day, we noticed how some men would go to the hills and dig holes there. During the evening the same men would stack thin naked corpses on boards and carry them away to the hills to be buried. So many bodies, so many wasted lives. Were these people not missed, somewhere? Did no one notice what was going on here?

We learned that only Polish prisoners were required to perform this "funeral" work, and perhaps this was a blessing. At least, as German prisoners, we did not have to take part in the "burial" of our own people!

We had also learned that most of the Polish people at this camp hated Germans and they were quite open about their hostilities. So it was no surprise to us that they did not protest about having to dispose of German corpses. I once overheard one of these Polish prisoners proclaim:

"We only make the holes large enough to cover their asses – let the wolves and jackals take care of the rest."

EAT TO LIVE!

After I had done this tree-felling work for several days, typhoid fever hit me as well. Typhoid fever is a terrible sickness. For me, it began with almost constant bloody diarrhoea. The fever then took my appetite away and I rejected even the little food that was given us. I was terribly weak and could not work.

The guards eventually brought me to the *lazarett*, a designated area in one of the barracks that took care of sick or injured prisoners. An older nurse tended to me and looked rather stern. I did not expect anything from her and closed my eyes in resignation. In the state I was in, I did not care about anything anymore.

When she came to take my temperature, she noticed that the soup beside my bed had not been touched.

"Why have you not eaten your soup?" She asked me in German.

In my feverish condition, it did not surprise me that she could speak my language. I was so weak and tired and it required too much effort to answer her, so I kept silent. Undeterred by my lack of interest, she continued:

"Do you want to die here, like the others? Do you want to be carried off to those hills, to be disposed of like rubbish? If you want to live, you must eat, *Margaretta!*"

She called me *Margaretta*. My name sounded interesting with her Russian accent. I was surprised that I had a name here. In this God-forsaken place! Where it seemed to me that humanity and compassion had died with the poor German prisoners who were concealed in the foothills of the Ural Mountains.

One of my captors had actually used my name! But perhaps I was wrong; perhaps she too, was here against her will. I was too weak to reason this out in my feverish mind. I did not have the strength to answer her. To simply thank her for caring about me. But I felt that I had found a friend. I opened my eyes a little.

The nurse was looking at me gravely, but I felt her empathy.

"You want to be able to go home again one day – so you must eat to get well! Eat *Margaretta!* Eat something!"

I looked into her eyes and saw that this stern-looking woman had a kind heart and meant well. Somehow, something in her made her treat me, a German prisoner, like a normal human being, as an individual who was suffering and in need of help. Her harsh surroundings and her experience at this camp had not corrupted her sense of compassion.

Even in my overwrought condition, I knew she was right. I had to eat if I wanted to survive. And I was grateful that someone seemed to care about me, so I tried to follow her advice. It was very painful, but I swallowed my soup. That night, I dreamed of returning to *Ostpreussen* and seeing my family and the little village of *Imten* again.

My "camp" friends visited me whenever they could. Their friendship and support had made the last weeks more tolerable at this camp. One evening, when Ruth came to the *lazarett* to visit, my condition was especially critical, because by then I was also combating pneumonia in addition to the typhoid fever.

Ruth was deeply religious and often quoted the scriptures while we worked piling lumber. But I did not want to listen to scriptures now.

"Take my clothes, Ruth," I whispered.

I was certain that I would not survive the night. I had nothing else to give, and I wanted Ruth to have something to make her life here a little more bearable.

Next to food, what would be most appreciated by a prisoner here? A change of clothing is an almost unobtainable luxury in a Russian camp! Ruth should have my clothes, I decided. For my final destination, I certainly would not need my clothes anymore, I reasoned in my feverish state.

"I will not take your clothes, Margarete! Because you aren't going to die! You have to live so that you can escape this God-forsaken place!" whispered Ruth passionately.

"And we are going back home again, together! You must live!" She said these words over and over again all through the night. This was probably the closest I came to death. Images of my family and friends in East Prussia swam in front of my eyes. I was so weak, so very tired. But Ruth had sparked something in me.

In my feverish state, I thought of home and of everything my family meant to me.

Yes, I want to go back home again. I need to go back home again. I don't want to be buried in the Ural Mountains. I don't want my body to end up as food for the hungry jackals and wolves. I don't want to stay in Russia! Yes ... I want to live! I will live!

Miraculously, from that night onward, I began to get my strength back. Perhaps I took comfort in knowing that I was not alone in the world. There seemed to be people who cared about my welfare and this gave me hope that there was still some good in this world, in spite of all the ugliness I had witnessed since January 23, 1945.

I do not know exactly how or why, but something gave me the will to carry on. That night, I sensed that some of my strength was returning and then I knew that I would not die in Russia. Even though I was still terribly sick, I knew that I would not die here.

Did the old Russian nurse take a special interest in me because I was German or did she see some sort of a kindred spirit in me? I only know that she always treated me with kindness. And she always worked diligently and efficiently, and I felt that she took a personal interest in my recovery. In this cold, bleak country, I actually mattered to someone.

She treated my pneumonia with glass bulbs that were placed on my back and though the procedure looked strange to me, it seemed to work. This kind-hearted nurse also came to my bed each night, watching over me. It made me feel secure somehow, that everything would be all right in the end.

There was another nurse at this *lazarett;* a younger woman of about twenty-five years of age. She was the extreme opposite of the gentle nurse who had helped me regain my strength. I felt alone and abandoned when she approached my bed in her arrogant and condescending manner.

This younger nurse made it quite clear that she was giving me, a lowly German prisoner, merely the minimum care required. She withheld even the slightest consideration, as if this would be superfluous here. When she was on duty, I missed the older nurse terribly and was fearful that she would not return.

What makes individuals so different from one another? I often pondered this question while I was in Russia. What made some people treat us with respect, even when there is no possibility of reward while others seemed to find a sadistic delight in tormenting the sick and helpless?

THE GIFT

There was a Polish grave-digger who was very kind to me during my time at the *lazarett*. He was a very serious-looking man and appeared to be about fifty years old.

For some inexplicable reason, he took an interest in my welfare. This was very unusual, since he was aware that I was German, so obviously this made him very different from the other grave-diggers. I knew that as grave-digger, this man had the opportunity to move more freely and to make contact with the surrounding Russian community. Since he was able to speak Russian, he could trade or make little deals to obtain a little extra bread or other food.

One day, to my surprise, the older nurse came to my bed and brought me a piece of bread that had been spread with lard. Lard was a rare luxury in this camp and a welcome relief from our monotonous and virtually "fat-free diet".

The nurse held the bread to me and said it was a gift from the Polish grave-digger. He continued to send bread to me in this manner several times and I was truly astonished because up until this time at this camp, I had experienced only the animosity of Polish people towards us.

This Polish grave-digger was actually going out of his way to help a sick German prisoner, when it would have been so easy to just ignore me. Again, it puzzled me, that people could be so different from one another.

THEFT

In the first months of our internment in Russia, some of us still had a few small personal articles that could be traded for potatoes or eggs. But this did not last long. As Germans, we were not permitted to move about outside the camp, but since the Polish grave-diggers were allowed this small freedom, I formulated a little plan. I would need the assistance of my "grave-digger friend" to carry out this plan.

I decided I would try my luck at "business" even though I was still confined to my bed. The next time the Polish grave-digger visited, I would show him my colourful shawl that I still had from *Ostpreussen*. Up to this time, I had always worn it hidden under my outer clothing. When I saw him again, I asked:

"Would you be able to trade this shawl for me?"

Even though I had made up my mind, I was still a little hesitant about giving it up. It was such a pretty piece of clothing, but I had nothing else of value anymore and I was hungry.

He accepted the shawl and was back in a few days with six potatoes, two carrots, and a couple of onions. The shawl was quickly forgotten when I enhanced my soup with the vegetables the grave-digger had brought. I had simply added these extra ingredients to my daily allotted *kasha*, but it tasted fresh and wonderful to me.

At death's door, I had truly wanted to give Ruth the clothing I still had tucked away, but I had survived typhoid fever and pneumonia and needed nourishment. What use is a pretty scarf to a prisoner, I reasoned. My appetite for food was back and I was very grateful to be alive, even in this strange cold place.

I decided to try my luck a second time with a nice dress that I had also kept hidden under my other clothing until now. I was so thin now, that I could wear several layers of clothing without being conspicuous.

While still in Germany, before the arrival of the Russian army, I had found a dress lying on the road and picked it up. Looking back on this event, I wonder now, what had been the fate of the owner of this dress?

But in the harsh camp atmosphere, I was becoming very practical. Russian women in this area had very few attractive clothes, as far as I was able to tell. Perhaps they would be willing to trade some food for something pretty to wear.

After my long illness, I was extremely hungry, and I was still hoping that I could get something extra to eat. More carrots, potatoes and onions to add to my watery *kasha*. It would be so wonderful, I thought. I dreamed that night of another tasty soup I would make with the vegetables that the Polish grave-digger would bring me.

But this time I would be disappointed. I am certain beyond a doubt, that the Polish grave-digger tried his best to help me but when he returned a few days later, he explained what had happened. There were tears in his eyes when he said:

"I am so sorry; the dress was stolen from me."

I had no reason to question his honesty. There were so many opportunities for theft in a prison camp. Nothing was safe, when everyone was hungry. How could I be angry with a "thief" for wanting to fill her stomach?

Theft among "comrades" was commonplace, but if Russian officers heard about it, the thief was punished and would have to spend a few days in a prison cell. The cell was actually a dark and dingy bunker with a dirt floor crawling with rats and mice.

Even a minor theft meant that the culprit would be lead through her own barracks, to set an example for other prisoners. She would be forced to repeat over and over again:

"I have stolen from my comrades."

This was a very humiliating and frightening experience, for both the perpetrator and the other prisoners who were forced to watch. How can they punish a girl for being hungry? Is it a crime to want to fill your stomach? The injustice of these public heart-rending demonstrations distressed us.

I was getting used to the pitiable meals again. It was always the same food, day in and day out. The same cup of millet or *kasha*, wet bread, and hot water for morning and the half litre of millet soup with hot water in the evening.

The entire daily bread ration was given in the morning but it never lasted the day because we were always too hungry to save it for later. In any case, we feared it would be stolen. In spite of our alarm when our own bread was stolen, most of us had pity for the thief. We understood that hunger makes thieves of almost everyone.

THE KIND NURSE INTERVENES

When I was released from the *lazarett*, I was ordered to go back to the barracks where I had been working up to the point where I got sick. I joined my friends and work comrades, who were overjoyed that I had survived typhoid fever and pneumonia. For now, we were all alive and we marvelled at our triumph over death because so many other women prisoners with whom we had worked had died already.

What lay ahead for me now? I knew that I would soon be going back to the old routine of rising at six o'clock in the morning and starting work two hours later in the woods. I dreaded this very much, because I still felt quite weak from my ordeal with typhoid fever and pneumonia.

At this camp, we had been classified according to our abilities for working under harsh prison conditions. Group One and Group Two were considered the best workers. Group Three and the "OK" Group were workers of lower value in the Russian prison camp system.

Most of the Group Three and "OK" workers were in actuality prisoners recently released from the *lazarett*. Now I belonged to this group. These weaker workers were generally assigned indoor tasks, or tasks which were not as demanding as felling trees and stacking logs.

To my astonishment and dismay, the Polish group leader wanted to assign me to tree-felling. But somehow the old Russian nurse must have heard that I was about to be assigned to hard labour. That same day, I saw her walk up to the group leader:

"How can you assign this girl to such hard work right away? She is still recovering from typhoid fever and pneumonia! I demand that she be put in the "OK" group until I inform you that she is ready for tree-felling!"

The Polish group leader had no choice but to follow her orders. I could not believe my ears. The old Russian nurse had come to my assistance once again! How had she known of my plight? What a relief for me! I was so thankful to her. How kind she was to me!

Her intervention on my behalf meant that I had a twenty-day "reprieve" of sorts. Under her authority, I was immediately given a notice, a slip of paper authorizing my re-classification as a "Group Three" prisoner.

It was very important to keep this slip of paper with me because each morning the Polish group leader went through the barracks, to make sure that no one was evading her responsibilities. I think it gave him great pleasure whenever he found a prisoner who had attempted to "shirk" her prison duties. It gave him an opportunity to menace someone.

For twenty days, I would have a lighter work load, but the work was still fairly strenuous for someone recovering from typhoid fever and pneumonia. Group Three or "OK" workers were obliged to scrub and clean the barracks. We were also responsible to see to it that our roommates made it to the "toilet" in time, so that the barracks were not soiled.

This was not as easy as it sounds, because diarrhoea was still pervasive and the "toilet" was almost four hundred meters from our camp. To travel that distance when plagued with severe diarrhoea required almost super-human self-control.

The large twenty meter deep hole that served as our collective "toilet" was a constant torment to us. Boards and planks lay across the hole and we had to be very careful not to lose our balance. The fear of plunging into the murky depth below was always there.

GRAVE-DIGGERS PROCESSION

Our unpleasant duty of "guarding" the poor souls plagued by the pain and inconvenience of diarrhoea coincided with the grave diggers schedule. Grave-diggers, as I mentioned earlier, buried the dead only at night. Perhaps the rationale was that the authorities did not want us to see how many German prisoners were dying at this camp.

But "Group 3" and the "OK Group" of prisoners saw everything. We were silent witnesses to the grave-diggers' procession.

Every evening, the grave-diggers passed right by us with their primitive "stretchers." These were just a few boards nailed together to carry the dead German prisoners to their final destination. The grave-diggers were able to easily carry six to eight bodies, because they were only skin and bones by then.

I will never forget these images. They still haunt me. Every evening, I would witness the same sad "funeral procession" and wonder about the families of these poor prisoners.

Sometimes, I was permitted to work in the bakery, which was much easier and certainly more pleasant. I also had the opportunity to work in the sewing room.

What would Mother say if she saw me now, sewing and mending the clothes of German prisoners? This is not quite what she had in mind for my apprenticeship!

But I was only able to work at these less demanding jobs for a little while, because my short twenty-day "reprieve" passed very quickly. In the back of my head was the dreary thought that very soon I would be joining the other girls and women and "normal" work.

I was very aware that my special circumstances were only temporary. The hard labour of felling trees and having to pile logs in meter high sections would not be postponed indefinitely. That was after all, the "normal" work of a German prisoner at this camp.

QUOTAS AND INTERROGATIONS

The exact degree of hardship experienced by prisoners depended upon the group leader. If he hated Germans, then he would simply inform the officers that you had not fulfilled your "quota." The reason why you had not been able to fulfill your quota did not matter.

The punishment for not fulfilling your quota was quite severe. Often, these women would be sent to the prison barracks for two or three days with almost nothing to eat. We, who had almost nothing to eat, could not imagine how it would be possible to survive with even less than "almost nothing to eat."

Did the Russians truly believe that food deprivation was a therapy for improving our ability to work? Could we expect to be treated differently in this insane environment? In any case, hunger dulled our capacity for rational thought. What was "normal"? What was "insane"? Who knew? We no longer questioned anything.

We remained at this camp until September. In the winter months, there would be no work for us at this camp, so new plans would have to be made for us, we learned. We did not look forward to this. The devil that we had grown accustomed to was easier to accept than the unknown.

One morning, we were ordered to assemble and were informed that we should collect all our belongings because we would not be coming back to this camp. So many thoughts raced through my mind.

Where to now? A better place? A worse place? Will they feed us better at the next camp? Russia is large. So very large. How many prisoners are there? How many camps are there?

Again, we were interrogated, as if this was a prerequisite to leaving Russian camps. All the standard questions were asked again:

"Where were you born?"

"Where did you live?"

"Was your father in the military?"

"Did he belong to the party?"

It took the whole day to interrogate us. When it started to get dark, the Russian officers said we should go back to our barracks, the trucks would come to collect us another day.

Before we could return to our quarters, the officers quickly inspected the barracks, to see if someone had left something of value behind. Something they could salvage for themselves. Their official airs always provided us with a little cynical entertainment.

Most of us hadn't really believed that we would be transported from the camp that day, because by then we knew all their tricks and had become accustomed to the delays that seemed to be a part of Russian prison life. This "inspection-interrogation" farce would repeat itself several times that month.

SECOND RUSSIAN CAMP

But one day towards the end of September, the trucks really did arrive and again we were herded away once more, like cattle into the backs of large trucks. It was not a pleasant drive to stand on the back of these trucks travelling along the bumpy Russian roads. It was very cold and we had to hold on to one another for support, so that we would not fall off of the truck.

Hours passed and then we arrived at our destination. This time, we would be quartered in a factory city. This was quite a change from the lumber camp that we had gotten used to.

In our new barracks, we were surprised to find actual beds! We would now have old iron beds that were equipped with flour bags stuffed with straw. In other words, these beds had "mattresses". This was a small improvement over the wooden planks that we had been sleeping on until now.

We later learned that the building was in fact a prison which had once housed Russian inmates. High fences surrounded the prison and again there were Russian guards stationed at all four corners. In front of the fence were several layers of barbed wire, but it did not alarm us anymore. We had gotten used to the sight of barbed wire.

The houses outside the fence were not without a certain attractiveness for Russian standards. This prison camp had several barracks. One of the barracks housed the kitchen, with tables where we could actually sit down to eat our *kasha* soups. The first camp did not have the luxury of tables. We had always eaten our rations standing.

THE "WASHING ROOM"

Beside the kitchen was a large "washing room" and de-lousing chamber. Every fourteen days, we were ordered to go to the washing room and there we would be given a bowl filled with water.

We were obliged to bundle our clothing and give these to an attendant, who would disinfect our clothes for us. In the summer we were given simple trousers and a shirt made from rough linen. In winter, we were given quilted pants and jacket, although these were little comfort when temperatures were below minus 35° Celsius.

We had to wait for about an hour or two to get our clothes back. Since the clothes we wore were the only clothes we possessed, we were forced to stand naked, side by side with the other girls and women until the clothes were available again. Standing there together, we noticed how much we had changed over the past year and how skinny we had all become.

Sometimes, when the clothing could not be disinfected quickly enough, for one reason or another, we had to wait longer to get our clothes back. Standing naked in front of strangers was miserable enough, but as the colder weather progressed, we shivered wretchedly, always under the watchful eyes of the guards.

One particularly bad day, we were forced to wait three hours. Russian winters can be terribly cold. One of the girls thought that we should try to sing to keep warm and it helped a little.

Unfortunately that day, the Polish *Kommandant* on duty was a mean-spirited man of about fifty years, who was known for mistreating German prisoners. Although the Russian administration officially segregated women from men, individual officers would often let the Polish male prisoners into the washing room, while we were still cleaning ourselves.

They pointed at us and laughed, and made jokes about how skinny we all were. We tried to ignore them, although no woman there would ever forget the looks of those callous men. We knew that the Polish prisoners were always given the less arduous tasks than the German prisoners and were given more food. Perhaps they felt superior to us for that reason. They were incapable of seeing us as human beings; they plagued us until we felt only despair and humiliation.

It amused them to see such awkward skinny German creatures standing naked in the middle of a washing room. We stopped our singing immediately, trying in vain to hide our shame and embarrassment from their malicious eyes.

I would learn much later that the Soviet Union did not sign the Geneva Prisoners of War Convention of 1929 until 1955. Perhaps this explains or reveals something. I don't know. Though we were also "prisoners of war" as German civilian prisoners in Russia in from 1945 to 1949, we did not seem to fit under the definitions and categories of the convention. We were a new category, a hidden category, a category without a name.

In any case, one article of the Convention states that non-combatants, combatants who have laid down their arms, and combatants who are *hors de combat* due to wounds, detention, or any other cause shall in all circumstances be treated humanely, including prohibition of outrages upon personal dignity, in particular humiliating and degrading treatment.

I find this particular article of the Convention most interesting, because we were obviously prisoners too. But we were forced to endure many outrages upon our personal dignity and "in particular humiliating and degrading treatment" in silence.

SILENT WITNESSES

In front of the camp was a small factory. Every morning, after breakfast, we were split into work crews of about forty to sixty women. Three or four officers were accommodated in a little house nearby, and would come out to count us before we trudged off to the factory.

Sometimes, it took them four tries before they got it right. Since we were always in groups of five, they only had to multiply the groups, but somehow they could not manage that. This was a small amusement for weary prisoners.

Deprived of any other intellectual stimulation, we privately made jokes about the absurdity of the situation and the mathematic bumbling of the Russian officers. Our enemy may have won the war, but how powerful was he really, when officers had not mastered simple mathematics?

Finally, when the counting was completed, we could exit the camp with our ever-present armed Russian guards. Every work-crew was accompanied by a Polish crew-leader who was called the "*Brigadier.*"

This Polish crew-leader would act as translator and supervisor. Whenever we paused in our work, to catch our breath a little, he shouted to us:

"What are you doing, standing still? Get moving!" We did not like him one bit.

How did the Geneva Convention define "humiliating and degrading treatment?" What criteria were used? How many kinds of cruelty is a human being capable of? I do not know the answers to these questions.

I only know that some of the Polish crew-leaders at our camp were incredibly brutal. Several of these crew-leaders had a special room to themselves, situated directly beside our own barracks.

Every evening, these Polish crew-leaders would force one or two male German prisoners into their room and beat these men until they bled from the inflicted wounds. We would cover our ears, but it could not drown out their ugly shrieking:

"Come on, you German pig, say *Heil Hitler* one more time!"

The Polish crew leaders had a lot of freedom, because late in the evening, the Russian officers had already left the premises. No one was there to witness what they did. Just female German prisoners and we did not count.

We knew of about ten crew-leaders who participated in these horrible beatings. Sadistic and savage do not express the cruelty the Polish crew leaders inflicted on defenceless old men. Oddly enough, they left women prisoners alone, but it was very painful for us to hear the screams and cries of those men.

These male German prisoners were no longer young. In fact, most of them were past fifty years of age and did not have any military connection.

The Polish crew leaders were aware that we knew what was going on. But they also knew that we were powerless. We could not stop them, we could not interfere.

We were too frightened ourselves to say anything. Who would listen to female German prisoners? Who would take pity on male German prisoners? We could only try to block out the sorrowful moaning of old men and cry ourselves to sleep.

During the war, many of these Polish crew-leaders had been in Germany and had learned our language then. I had seen prisoners of war in *Ostpreussen,* since our region had also housed them. Only we had treated our prisoners very differently. They also worked on farms or factories, but were able to move about quite freely and were fed at least as well as the Germans who housed them.

There are always exceptions, of course. But on the whole, they were treated far better than the way we were treated in Russia. Why were we treated so badly? We could not understand it. The war was over. What right, what permission did the Russians have, to take German women and children away from their homes, and force them into slave labour?

Had the world really become this heartless and cold since the end of the war? Why were Russians allowed to degrade us, to deprive us of even minimal human comforts? We were civilians; we had nothing to do with the war. Was there no humanitarian organization watching? Was there no one at all willing to help us?

BLESSINGS AND RUMOURS

There was one small blessing for us at this second camp. It seemed that the typhoid crisis seemed to have finally ended. Sadly, the weaker women and girls had died, but the survivors had gotten used to the conditions, the lack of adequate food and even the hard work.

Through our work, we frequently had contact with women who worked in other crews and so were able to trade information and learn about what was going on in the surrounding area.

We found out that conditions were similar for these other women too, and realized that the capacity for human beings to adapt to almost any situation is astonishing, if not almost infinite. This recognition was a reason to rejoice a little.

We are adapting. We are surviving. We are surviving because we have learned to adapt to insane inhumane conditions.

Towards the end of 1946, every once in a while we would hear rumours that a truck was coming for us, and that we were going home soon. At first we believed this, but we were disappointed again and again, when we found out that it was not true.

But still, the thought of transportation coming to this isolated camp gave us a little hope. We kept thinking *maybe*. Maybe is a word of hope.

Maybe this time the truck will come for us. Maybe the next truck will take us home. Maybe I will see my family again.

You can live a long time on a little hope. In any case, we all had difficulty believing that the Russians would keep us here forever. Slavery had been abolished, hadn't it? Surely someone, somewhere would bring the world's attention to our plight?

RUSSIAN COAL

The work at this camp kept us very busy and there was more variety in the type of work we were to do. Sometimes we would lay railroad tracks, other days we would unload cement bags or heavy rocks from large transport trucks. Such hard work and so little to eat! I don't know how we managed, as malnourished as we were.

We were given more food than at the beginning of our internment, but it was still so inadequate. The winters were especially hard. Even when the temperature fell to -35° Celsius, we were still required to work our regular eight to ten hours outside. On an almost empty stomach. We were not fed more on colder days.

We tried to organize ourselves in different ways and it became evident that necessity was also our "mother of invention". We soon realized that if we brought a few pieces of coal with us to work, we could make a little fire to warm ourselves in the woods. There was always enough brush around to keep our fire going throughout the day. In this way we could warm our hands and feet a little while we worked.

Our guards permitted us this little luxury, mainly because they benefited from the fire as well. They probably suffered from the cold more than we did, simply because other than watching us, they had nothing else to do.

To our surprise, sometimes certain officers felt sorry for us and would let us stay indoors, when the weather was too severe. It had to be colder than -35° Celsius though, otherwise we would not qualify for this "holiday."

The coals came from a factory that was quite close to our camp and there were huge quantities of coal stored there. The prisoners who worked at the factory, always tried to hide a piece of coal under their jackets to bring back to the camp.

If the guards noticed that one of the women had a piece of coal under her clothing, it would be confiscated. If the whole crew was found to be carrying stolen coal, sometimes the guards would point their rifles upward and fire several times to scare us.

But the biting cold was stronger than any fear we may have had and we continued the practice. Whenever we had the opportunity, we brought a little bit of coal back with us. Even though it was considered stealing, we needed this coal to survive the winter and we did not stop taking it, even under threat of punishment. Russian coal was very good. It was about forty to sixty centimetres long and heated very well.

We were aware that the Russian guards would also steal coal from the factory whenever they had the opportunity and possibly for this reason, they would sometimes let us go, knowing full well that we had hidden a piece under our clothing.

CHRISTMAS 1946

By the end of 1946, many of the Russian guards were not quite so severe with German women prisoners. Perhaps it is more difficult to mistreat people when you see them on a daily basis. Or perhaps they had orders from elsewhere to be more lenient with us now. In any case, we noticed that there was a change.

But the lack of food and the hard working conditions did not improve and we were still prisoners, restricted and forced to accept whatever came our way.

We were also very dependent on the unpredictable nature of our "transportation system". For example, on some days, the trucks did not arrive to collect us after our work day was over. This meant that we had to walk the five to eight kilometre distance back to camp again. After a long and hard work day, this was an added burden.

On the other hand, the alternative of standing on the back of a truck in freezing cold weather with the wind whipping your face was not very pleasant either. Working outside the entire day, our bodies had acclimatized somewhat to the temperature, and on some days walking back to camp was sometimes preferable. Even though we were exhausted when the work day ended.

At this camp, we were again separated into the standard Group 1, Group 2 Group 3 and "OK" groups. This seems to have been the standard procedure of categorizing prisoners at other internment camps as well, I would learn later.

Again, "Group Three" and "OK" groups would stay behind and take care of camp duties. When we got back to camp, everything was prepared for the evening, and our quarters were warmed up already. This too, was a small blessing.

In December of 1946, the Russian officers permitted us to bring three pine trees into the camp so that we could celebrate Christmas a little. The male German prisoners who worked in the metal shop had brought us little metal shavings and cuttings which we transformed into "Christmas ornaments" for our trees. The light reflecting from the shiny metal hanging from the pine trees brightened our lives a little. That too, gave us hope.

We had placed the pines in our mess hall and it cheered us and we thought of our families back in Germany.

Did they survive the war? Were they celebrating Christmas? What were they doing? What were they eating for their Christmas dinner? Where they thinking of us?

That year, we were also allowed to prepare a short theatrical presentation. Surprisingly, some of the Russian officers actually attended our Christmas play with their families! There were some very talented women among us, who were capable of writing quite entertaining theatre pieces.

1947

By 1947, conditions at the camp had stabilized somewhat and the women who had survived the first years in Russia seemed to be stronger now, despite the limited food. Perhaps the old adage that "what doesn't kill you makes you stronger" really is true.

I had learned over the years to accept the situation for what it was and had realized right from the start that the only way to survive in Russia was to work to the best of my ability. I never tried to evade the work that I was required to do, and no one refused to work with me because of clumsiness on my part or for not pulling my own weight. Complete work participation was still very important under the dreaded Russian "quota" system.

My docile acceptance of and conformity to this situation did not mean I had given up my hope that a truck would come for us one day, to take us back home. I longed to see Grandmother and Mother and my Aunt Hanna and my sister and cousins. I hadn't seen them since late autumn in 1944. So long ago! Were they still alive?

In the spring of 1947 we were finally given permission to receive mail. This was a real luxury for people who had been deprived of all printed material for over two years! I could hardly believe this was true.

Communication! Permission to write words, expressions, thoughts, feelings. A link to the outside world. A link to our families.

Of course it was only possible to receive mail if you wrote someone first. We were given small postcards, but you had to have an address to send your postcard to. This was a problem for some prisoners.

Luckily, I had remembered the mailing addresses of two relatives. I was very good at remembering addresses because I had always been the "official letter writer" for my family. Hoping he would still be alive, I wrote first to my grandfather's brother in Berlin — my Uncle Arthur.

I addressed the other postcard to my Aunt Frieda's sister in *Bottrop*. I remembered that this had been Aunt Frieda's intended destination, but we were separated when I had been taken prisoner by the Russian soldiers in *Bublitz*. So of course I had no way of knowing if she had actually made it to *Bottrop*. Had she survived? How could I know? But I took a chance anyway and wrote to my Aunt Frieda, in care of her sister.

We were all probably presumed dead or missing, so we imagined what a shock it would be for family members who would finally hear that we were still alive — and so far away in Russia!

About four months later, I was thrilled to get an answer. Aunt Frieda had not been able to write very much because the text was strictly limited to what would fit on a post card. The Russian authorities obviously wanted to keep an eye on our correspondence.

Communication was not quite as free as I had hoped for, but there was enough space on the postcard to let me know that Grandmother, Mother, Helga, Aunt Hanna and my cousins were alive. I was so very happy — I could think of nothing else that day. What a relief it was to know that my family was alive and that they now knew that I was alive too. Far away in Russia — but alive!

I would learn later that with the assistance of the Red Cross, Aunt Frieda had managed to track down all our family members. This was very fortunate for me, and I will always be very grateful that Aunt Frieda had not given up in her search to find me. In the chaos of post-war Germany, this had not been easy. I considered myself extremely lucky. Not everyone at my camp was able to find a "contact" in Germany.

About a month after her first reply, Aunt Frieda wrote again to tell me that after my release, I should come to live with her. This too, was wonderful news. But when would the Russian authorities release German prisoners?

Soon after my second postcard reply from Aunt Frieda, I also received a reply from Uncle Arthur. His postcard confirmed that my family was alive but sadly informed me that two of my uncles had died in the war. My favourite uncle had died on May 8, 1945, just as the war ended. He had not lived to see his fortieth birthday. Even if I get out of Russia, I will never see Uncle Albert again, I thought sadly.

THIRD CAMP: "FREE" WORKERS

In October of 1947 we were transported to another camp, where oil pipelines were being laid. Here, our duties consisted of digging trenches for these pipelines. They had to be excavated to a depth of about four meters, which is very difficult when all you have is a shovel. Usually, we just dug earth, which was strenuous enough, but sometimes we had to pull out rocks as well.

For eight hours, we would be required to stand in these trenches and shovel. The deeper we dug, the harder it was to throw the soil. We soon figured out it would be a little easier if we created a "platform" about half way so that the person at the lowest level would only have to throw the earth about half the distance up to that "platform" and the worker stationed there would only have to throw the soil the remaining distance.

It was a very primitive solution, but we had no other tools, no other means. It seemed idiotic to do this work in the winter. It was difficult enough shovelling the soil in the autumn, but in winter the snow would just blow right back in our faces as we shovelled.

Sometimes there were snow storms, but still we had to work at these pipelines. It looked as though they had no other work for us. Maybe it didn't really matter what we did, as long as we were outside, working the obligatory eight hours and some sort of prescribed quota system was fulfilled. Russian prison logic eluded us.

At this new camp, we were informed that from now we were considered "free" workers. What an odd terminology to describe people who were still being held in Russia against their will!

In any case, we would now receive a few *roubles* for our labour. Unfortunately, there was a drawback to our new "freedom". We now had the added responsibility of having to pay for our "accommodation."

We were now permitted to leave the camp and make our little food purchases at the *bazaar*. The money that we received for our labour was enough to pay for a few potatoes and some bread.

Unfortunately our "wages" were always paid out about a week or two later and often our "wages" were several days late. Under this new "payment for accommodation" system, how could we purchase our food when our payment was late?

It was impossible to save our hard-earned *roubles,* since what we earned was just enough to pay for a little food. We had no other choice but to go among the Russian villagers and beg for food.

Sadly, these Russians had very little food themselves. We would see them come to work with a little bit of bread and some potatoes which they would warm in the ashes of a fire. It always surprised us to see that our "enemy" did not have all that much to eat either.

If we went to their homes, knocking on their doors, asking if they could spare a little bread for a hungry prisoner, most gave us something, even though we could see that they did not have much.

They also know how it feels to be hungry, we realized. It was an embarrassment for us to have to beg, especially from poor people, but we were so hungry. Pride does not feed an empty stomach.

If the *roubles* were more than three days late, then we were allowed to stay at the camp. The Russian officers must have realized by now that "performance" would be severely hampered when a worker has had almost nothing to eat for three days.

So we continued to beg for food. Our success in finding something to eat among this population demonstrated to us that some of these Russians had sympathized with German prisoners. Some would even ask us:

"Why are you still in Russia? The war is over!"

"The war may be over, but not for German prisoners in Russia." we would reply.

COOKING

This camp had two large cooking fields in the communal kitchen. By this time, we had our own make-shift pots and cooking utensils. My pot was actually a small pail that one of the German prisoners had modified for me. As soon as we came back from work, we raced to get our pots on the cook top.

Because we always came back hungry and wanted to make our meals was quickly as possible, before the other work-crews arrived, we did not always examine our pots closely enough.

Once when I turned to stir my soup, I was horrified to see three dead mice floating in the middle of my *kasha*. It turned my stomach, but I could not throw out the only pot I owned. What else would I use to cook my meal? My only choice was to discard everything and start over. I simply boiled water in the pot several times before I would use it again. Dinner was very late that night and I had a smaller meal than what I had planned.

It took a lot of ingenuity to make a meal from the few *roubles* that we got paid. How many different meals can you make with just bread and potatoes or *kasha*? We did not have much else. Usually, we just grated some potatoes and boiled this into a "soup." The bread was eaten dry.

Sometimes the neighbouring Russian women would come to our fence, offering to sell us an apple or *perogies*. Fruit, other than apples, was not common to this region; at least I had never seen Russians carrying other fruit with them.

Potatoes, onions, carrots and *perogies* were sold near our camp at the *bazaar* and whenever we had a little free time we would walk through the various stands to see what was available for a few *roubles*. But even these simple vegetables and food items were often beyond our reach; the few *roubles* we were paid did not stretch that far.

Though I was still always hungry, I often reflected that it was so strange that few people got sick after 1947. It was as though all those prisoners who had survived past the first two years in Russia were immune somehow to further suffering. We were still almost always hungry and yet in some bizarre way, we were relatively "healthy."

The Polish male prisoners who had been so hateful to us earlier seemed to be gone now. Perhaps they had been able to return to

Poland. And there was a definite change in attitude towards us. We could not help noticing this on an almost daily basis.

Perhaps this was a good sign. Perhaps something was finally working in our favour, we thought. We often wondered against hope, whether someone, somewhere was finally taking measures to free us from this strange confinement in Russia. Some prisoners were pessimistic, most of us were puzzled.

Germany has lost the war, why should we matter anymore? Everyone has forgotten us by now. But why have the Russian authorities suddenly given us permission to write postcards to our relatives?

We did not understand why the Russians were treating us differently. It was all a mystery to us. Again, we heard rumours that we would be released soon. We waited and waited but nothing happened.

FRIENDSHIP

At this camp, women were permitted to have male friends. They were usually from the adjoining male prison. Sometimes these prisoners would come to our camp to sleep with their women friends. Alternatively, some women would go to the male prisoner camp. But the latter case was not as common.

Often, this was simply an attempt to improve one's situation by sharing resources or to obtain a little more food in "quasi-marriages". These arrangements were perfectly understandable. It is only human to seek love and comfort. Especially under our circumstances, in such a bleak place, so far away from home.

I also had a male friend at this time, a very nice young man. We were together for about three weeks, when he politely asked if he could move in with me. He earned a few more *roubles* than I was earning at the time and was therefore able to buy more food.

In spite of my terrible experience at the hands of the Russian soldiers, I still believed that I ought to be married before sleeping with a man. My upbringing had been very strict, and I would never have considered challenging the beliefs I had grown up with.

I was also very afraid of becoming pregnant. Perhaps I need not have been afraid, because, to my knowledge, none of the German women prisoners experienced menstrual periods during their time in Russia.

We often discussed this situation with each other. *Why don't we have normal menstrual periods anymore? Are they putting something in our food? Will we be normal again someday? Will we still be able to have children?*

In fact, in my own case, my menstrual periods did not normalize again until about a year after I was back home in Germany.

So I politely declined his advances for the reasons I have mentioned. I should add that I also did not want to fall in love with someone, not knowing what the future would bring. What would be the fate of German prisoners in Russia? Where would we end up? How can a prisoner really make plans for a future?

My friend was a very good looking man and I would probably still recognize him today. I did not see him again, but I often wonder what happened to him. Was he able to return to Germany?

This situation was also complicated by the fact that a Lithuanian woman of about fifty-five years shared my sleeping quarters, and I had to take her feelings into consideration. She worked in an office because she was very fluent in Russian.

TRIBUTE TO MY FRIENDS

The Lithuanian woman's family name was Mueller, coincidentally the same family name as my own, and she treated me as a daughter. She was a very kind woman and I liked her very much. We became friends.

I made many friends during my time in Russia, but Inge, Eva, Renate, Waltraud and Ruth were especially dear to me. We were fortunate to have found each other almost right from the beginning—since those fearful days in *Bublitz*. Their friendship made the ugliness of camp life more bearable, especially during the early years.

Inge, a young woman about my age, usually slept in the cot above me. She was very pretty but not very practical and always had great difficulty begging for or stealing food, even though our survival depended on obtaining food wherever possible. Whenever a Russian woman gave her bread, Inge was overjoyed that she had a little extra food to share with us.

"In Russia, even dried bread tastes like cake." she would proclaim whenever she succeeded in finding a bit of extra bread.

Both her parents had been brutally shot to death before her eyes by Russian soldiers. Her father had tried in vain to defend his daughter so they had shot him. Then they shot her mother. I will never forget her. She had hoped to return to Berlin someday and wanted to become a teacher. I do not know if she did. I hope so.

Eva, from Pomerania, was also a special friend for too brief a time. Tragically, Eva died of typhoid fever, right at the beginning of our internment, at the first camp. She had been mistaken for dead and the Polish grave-diggers had been ready to bury her, when she suddenly sprang to life. Perhaps she too, did not want to die in Russia. But the typhoid fever was too strong and she had been too close to death. She had clutched for life one more time to escape from her desolate surroundings, but it was in vain. Her body too, lies somewhere in the Ural Mountains.

Renate! I still see her face before me. She was a beautiful young woman with clear blue eyes and light blond hair. A very quiet person, she often sang softly to herself while stacking lumber or shovelling soil. It was her way of blocking out the bleak landscape that confronted us every day.

Waltraud was always cheerful — even when there was so little to be cheerful about and her wit and good humour raised our spirits on more than one occasion. She was an excellent story teller and back then I often told her:

"Waltraud, you must write this down, our story needs to be told. When you go back home, when you go back to work in your family's photography shop, you must take the time to write of our experiences."

Of course, I can never forget Ruth, who came to visit me in the *lazarett* and tried so hard to help me overcome typhoid fever and pneumonia. Her prayers helped me survive that dark perilous night, when death seemed so certain. When death seemed like a welcome release. Courageous Ruth, whose concern for a friend was stronger than her fear of typhoid fever.

LONGING FOR FREEDOM

We had a Hungarian crew-leader now, a man of about forty-five years, who supervised us at the work site and served as translator whenever Russian officers came to check on us. He slept in our barracks in one corner by the door, and he did not touch any of the women, as far as I know.

He often defended us, stepping in to correct the situation when something was amiss with our quotas, or when our few *roubles* pay did not arrive on time. This happened quite frequently and without these precious *roubles*, we could not buy food.

The Hungarian crew-leader must have taken pity on the "free workers" with empty stomachs. When he saw that we had gone two or three days with almost no food, he would not force us to go out to work. He was a kind soul and did his best, in this God-forsaken place.

So the weeks and months passed with a certain predictability and soon another year and a half was gone. The monotony was stifling. Always the same work, always the same food. Every day just dry bread, water, potato or *kasha* soup. No butter, no seasonings, no meat, all this time!

In the summer, we felt fortunate when we found mushrooms. Of course, we had to be very cautious and make sure they were not poisonous. The Russian villagers took the trouble to warn us, so we soon learned to select just the edible ones. Sometimes, we would collect nettles and cook these into a sort of "spinach". The nettles added a little iron and variety to our bland diet.

GOING HOME IN 1949

We reflected that prisoners who survived those terrible first years in Russia were no longer plagued with lice, bedbugs or other parasites. These pests had been with us since our arrival in Russia and now they were leaving us alone. What a blessing that was!

"We must be immune to just about everything now," we said to ourselves. Perhaps we were.

Dealing with the monotony was another matter. Day in and day out we dug trenches. Even in winter. Our time was spent fulfilling "quotas"—the mysterious foundation to the economic system in Russia.

One day, about the middle of October 1949, the Hungarian crew leader came to our barracks and said:

"I have good news for you today. You are all going back to Germany. After tomorrow, you will no longer be working here and you are all getting fourteen days rest before your departure."

For some reason, even though our hopes had been dashed so many times by his predecessors and by rumours that constantly floated around the camp, we believed the Hungarian crew leader.

At least the part about not having to work was true. Every morning from that day on, we were called to assemble outside. We did not understand at the beginning, but we soon realized what was happening. The Russians were making a final selection from our group. This meant that some of us would be going home at last, but sadly, some would have to remain behind.

We followed this selection process very closely. One woman, about fifty years of age, who had been involved in a political organization, was taken away. A younger woman who had been a guard in a Rumanian prison camp in Germany, and a young boy who had been born in Russia, but whose mother was from the western part of Germany were also removed from our particular group.

Where are they taking these people? What will happen to them?

THE SELECTION PROCESS

This "sorting out" of candidates for freedom went on for several days.

Are they going to keep some people from leaving? Will they be forced to remain in Russia forever? What about us? Will we be able to leave?

We whispered our fears to each other. Everyone was worried, now that the end to our imprisonment seemed to be so close. We were so worried that we would be forced to stay in Russia forever. It is terrible to be at the mercy of what seemed to be such arbitrary decision-making. We were not in a position to defend our case or anyone else's case. We were forced to accept whatever decision was made for us.

Then one day, this gruelling selection process was over. No other people were removed from our group. It was finally happening, we learned. What we had waited for so long. We were going "home" again!

But we had been away from our country for almost five years! We had other concerns now. Where was "home?"

What would our lives be like at "home?" What was Germany like now — almost five years after the war? Would we recognize our country? Would our families recognize us?

We said our tearful goodbyes to those who were forced to stay in Russia. This was very difficult for me. I knew so many of them. We had spent so many years working, eating, sleeping, crying, and worrying together. The separation would be difficult, because over the years, our friends in this prison had become like family to us.

We noticed that many of the women condemned to stay in Russia, were women who had never had to do hard physical labour before their arrival here. They had come from more privileged classes; they were people who had been able to hire workers to handle menial chores for them.

Why must they stay in Russia? Why are they being treated differently?

However, in my experience, these "privileged" women had often surprised us with their strength and courage. They worked as hard as we did, trying to fulfill the work quotas that were set for us and worked extra hard so that they would not let their particular group down. How would they manage now? Without us, they were now entirely alone in Russia. In this culture that would always be so foreign to us.

NEW CLOTHES

We were still owed some *roubles* for our work and we were asked to exchange this money for new trousers and a quilted jacket. This was an unexpected generosity, even if we had to pay for them with our own labour. Our first new clothes in all these years!

We were very grateful for the trousers and quilted jacket. It was October and in this region already quite cold.

"We want you to look neat and orderly when you arrive in Germany," the Russian officers said to us.

Did they really mean this? Was this a strange Russian pride? Or perhaps it was their way of saying:

"Here you are, Germany! We give you your people back, as good as new!"

Well, we weren't as good as new, but at least our clothes were new.

New trousers and jacket for almost five years of our lives! But we knew it was foolish to dwell on this when we were already focussed in another direction. From now on we looked westward. At least and at last, we were going home. To Germany.

There was one man, a German prisoner who had been there since 1914, who offered to make me a little suitcase for a few *roubles*. I did not really have any belongings to put in this suitcase, but I was happy to give my remaining *roubles* to him. I was very sad that he had to stay behind. What had he done, that condemned him to a life in Russia — away from his own country, away from his family?

Again, we were packed into large trucks, headed for the trains. We huddled together and thought back to that terrible time, over four years ago when we came from the west, not knowing what was to become of us. Now, as survivors, we still could not believe that we would really be going home again.

We were filled with apprehension and confusion. So much time had passed. What was Germany like now? What would our loved ones say when they saw us? We thought about this constantly and discussed our feelings openly with each other.

Any day now, the Russian officers would come and say it was all a mistake; we would be staying after all. They were not known for keeping their word. Would the train suddenly stop at another camp? Would the officers laugh and say:

"It was all a joke, you are staying in Russia!"

Now homeward bound, we had endless discussions about these possibilities. As prisoners in Russia for so many years, we had learned to always expect the worst.

In the last four years I had often dreamed of our house in *Ostpreussen*. The whole family would be sitting around that old wooden table, with our old faded dishes and I would be so happy to see all the familiar objects I had grown up with.

Then I would open my eyes and the grey dreariness of my prison would jolt me back to my sad reality. I was still in Russia after all. Would I wake from this "dream" and find out that I would stay here forever? Condemned to be a prisoner in Russia for always, like that poor German prisoner who had been here since 1914?

TRAVELLING WESTWARD

I am actually on a train, and I am travelling west! I am really travelling back to Germany, after so many years! The day I had thought would never come! I am finally leaving the misery of the Russian prison camps behind. I reflect on our "accommodations" and I joke with my friends:

"Accommodations seem to be much better this time!"

They laugh at my little joke. At least it seemed like the kasha soups and hot water "tea" tasted better. Renate, Ruth, Waltraud and Inge are still with me after all this time, which seems like another miracle to me. We talk excitedly about our "future plans"—an expression we have not used in a very long time. There is a future.

We are even given a little "preview" of freedom. The guards permit us to get off the train for short periods of time. We are unaccustomed to this freedom — it seems so peculiar to us.

Of course, we have to be careful not to wander too far from the train. We are not always sure when exactly the train would start moving again. Often the train starts while some women are still outside. They have to run swiftly to catch up with the train. Quickly we rush to the door, stretch out our arms and pull them back inside the train again. We do not want anyone on this train to stay in Russia!

It happened to me once and this scared me so much, I was very careful afterwards. I did not want to be left behind! Certainly not now when freedom was so near! What a strange feeling to be running after a train that is headed back to the homeland you were forced to leave so long ago!

"TEMPORARILY UNFIT"

Our train was quite long and there were even a few cars filled with male German prisoners. We only discovered this a few days later as we began to explore the train. Having so much in common, we quickly made new friendships and exchanged addresses, promising to write when we got "home."

Every day, Germany was closer, and the excitement in the train grew more intense with each kilometre. Travelling through Poland, we were shocked to see that everything still looked quite devastated. We had expected that five years after the war, everything would have been restored to a certain extent. This made us apprehensive.

In Germany's "Soviet zone" there seemed to be more order, but tremendous poverty. We could see that general goods and food and clothing were extremely hard to obtain. Children in rags followed us constantly, begging for bread. What a surreal image — hungry survivors of the war begging from hungry survivors of a Russian prisoner camp.

In *Friedland*, the designated refugee camp, we were all given a thorough physical examination by American doctors. My certificate of discharge was stamped "TEMP UNFIT" which at that time I did not know was an English abbreviation for "temporarily unfit." I weighed 42 kilos on the day of my examination at this refugee camp.

I still wonder today, about that casual terminology for describing how those years in Russia had left their mark on my body, on my soul. "Temporary" seems to suggest that the doctors knew that I would be completely well again, soon. Did they really know this?

"LOOKING LIKE VAGABONDS"

Everyone was given forty DM, but we were obliged to spend this money in the eastern sector of Germany. I spent some of my money on three herrings and a loaf of bread, which I devoured the same evening. How wonderful to have something other than *kasha* and water! It is impossible to describe this feeling to people who have never known what it is to be hungry.

The women who worked at this refugee camp told us that we could not go to the western sector of Germany looking like vagabonds, and we were given a set of new clothes. I think that vagabonds would not have been as skinny as we were then. Still, I was the possessor of two new sets of clothing in such a short time! No one had cared how we looked for such a long time.

They were not exactly new, most likely donated clothing from charity organizations. Nevertheless, they were in good condition and it was such a pleasure to be able to wear a coat and dress again. It had been such a long time, since I had been able to dress like a woman.

We were directed to go to various departments where we were asked all sorts of questions. For example, what type of work we had done in Russia, or if we were able to indicate on a map the last camp where we had worked, or if we knew how many prisoners had died at the camp.

After this interrogation, we were told that we should contact our next of kin and ask if they would be willing to provide accommodation. I wrote my Aunt Frieda immediately and in a few days her response came and it was positive, as I had expected, since she had already invited me earlier. I was family and in those days, family members accepted this kind of responsibility, no questions asked.

TRAIN TO FLENSBURG

The response from my aunt was official proof, that I had accommodation. Now I could request permission to leave the refugee camp. Clutching the letter from my Aunt Frieda, I headed immediately for the authorities. I now had my passport to freedom.

I received a *"Heimkehrerschein"* and with this I was able to get a train ticket to *Flensburg*, in northern Germany, where my Aunt Frieda lived. I did not know much about *Flensburg* and wondered what it was like there. Would it be like East Prussia?

On the train to *Flensburg,* I had so much time to think. What did I think about? Images of food flooded my mind; all the wonderful meals I would be able to enjoy again. Again, and again persistent thoughts of food — just as it had been for most prisoners for all those years in the Russian camps! Would I always think about food?

I mused about how after work, we would quickly pick mushrooms and then try to clean them before the darkness made it impossible to see what we were doing. Outside, sometimes as late as ten o'clock at night we would cook them. We didn't have salt or any method of preserving mushrooms, so we tried to keep whatever was left over for our soup the next day.

Unfortunately, by that time, they were often covered in maggots! But we learned not to care. We simply fished the maggots out and kept on eating. Greedily, devouring every last bit because we were so hungry. We came to accept our situation, whatever came our way, because we knew we did not have the power to change anything. An odd combination of powerlessness, acceptance and adaptation was what enabled us to survive in Russia.

But we thought about food constantly! We even dreamed of food when we slept on those hard wooden planks. We held long discussions about food and food preparation, exchanging stories of how our mothers prepared different foods. What were our favourite recipes? Our favourite vegetables? Our favourite fruits?

We played countless games where food was the central theme. Name ten foods that start with "s." What herbs were most often used by our mothers? What were the names of different flavours? Could we describe a flavour? What did different foods taste like, how did they smell? What kind of texture did they have? One of my favourite foods was dumplings, I had said once. So we strained our culinary memory for all the different ways of making dumplings. We would have the same discussions about omelettes, breads, puddings and any other foods we could think of.

We thought back to what was for us "the good old days" when there was enough food for us, and so much variety! The watery *kasha* and soggy bread in the Russian camps always left us craving for more food. We longed for even the simplest fare of our childhood. Potatoes! Beans! Bread! Milk! Those simple foods seemed like extravagant luxuries to us in Russia.

My train stopped in *Hamburg* and here I was greeted by four nurses from the Red Cross. I could see many other people at the station, holding up photographs of their children or relatives, and they would ask passersby if anyone had seen their son or daughter, or husband or father or uncle. They looked so hopeful and yet fearful as well.

What can be worse, than not knowing whether a dear family member is still alive? It was heartbreaking to see these people clutching their photographs, hanging on to a little shred of hope.

As the trained moved on towards *Flensburg,* memories would flash back of my fellow prisoners, who had died like flies in the first year of our imprisonment, in the cold prison camps of Russia.

Their skinny naked bodies had been dumped into holes somewhere in *Ufa*, somewhere in the foothills of the Ural Mountains, somewhere in Russia. Would someone go there one day, to recover them? Was there anyone left to care about them?

GUARDIAN ANGELS

I wondered what happened to those terrible Russian soldiers who committed atrocities against German women. Did they ever reflect on the suffering they inflicted? Did the "anonymity" of war or the atmosphere of revenge give these individuals the right to treat us the way they did?

Many Russians had lost a brother or a father in this war but this could never excuse the sadistic actions and senseless raping of German girls and women. War, unfortunately breeds hatred and there was so much hatred then. Especially towards Germans. But it still does not justify what the Russians did to us.

Why did others reject this "victor's right" and treat us as humans? After all, we were the enemy, and they did not have to treat us humanely, judging by the general atmosphere of those first years in Russia. But they did.

Regardless of what others said or did. Or did not do.

I will never forget the cruel Polish crew leaders and how callously they treated German prisoners. I can understand how the thirst for revenge can sometimes cloud judgment. What I do not understand is the deliberate tormenting of an innocent human being. Someone who has no means of escape.

But I will always remember the Polish farmhand who had saved my life from the Russian soldiers, and the kind Polish grave-digger who had brought me food when I was dying from typhoid fever, and that wonderful Russian nurse who took care of me when I had typhoid fever, and the Hungarian crew leader who treated us with dignity. In my mind, these were unforgettable acts of kindness in a ruthless environment.

Leaning back in my seat, I tried to concentrate on the positive aspects of the past years, because in spite of everything, I had survived! So many others had died at the Russian prisoner camps, but I had survived! This was more important to me than anything else. Miraculously, I had escaped death so many times since that winter in 1944.

What a strange revelation it had been for me to discover in Russia that it was not always the apparently strong individuals that survived. That is the mystery of life and death. I am convinced that there was another force another at work, behind the scenes, a hidden, inexplicable, unfathomable power.

There but for the grace of God, I reflected. I had surely felt God's grace. This thought went through my head repeatedly while I looked out the train window. I had been so very lucky. Perhaps I also had a guardian angel watching over me all the time. Or many guardian angels, because it would have been too much work for just one angel to protect me in *Ostpreussen* in the winter of 1944 and all those years in the Russian prison camps after that. Maybe that old Russian nurse was just one of many guardian angels who watched over me.

I was a young, inexperienced girl, barely eighteen years old when I arrived in Russia. I no longer felt young, and I had learned too well about the fragility of life.

Eat or starve. That had been the prisoner's guiding faith and philosophy. Regardless of what was served before you. Regardless of what fate brings. *Eat to survive.* The Russian nurse had told me this when I had needed to hear it most.

Survival was a gift and this gift had given me an appreciation for life far greater than I would have had, if I had lived protected in some safe haven for the last five years. This too, I had learned in Russia. In some crazy way, I was grateful to Russia for making me a much stronger person than I was before.

I had been raised with the notion that your true worth as a human being is what you do when you know that no one is watching you. The years in Russia confirmed my beliefs. There must have been others who felt this way, even in Russia, and those were the people who had helped me to survive.

There was no one watching when the old Russian nurse helped me, and there was no one watching when the Polish grave-digger brought me bread. They were not rewarded for treating me kindly. Yet, they, along with many others chose to be kind to German prisoners. These people chose to act humanely, even though they did not have to.

The ordinary Russians villagers I met, especially during the last two years, actually lived in deplorable poverty. But I was continually surprised by their generosity and humanity. Often they would tear a piece of their last slice of bread to share it with a hungry German prisoner.

Were these Russians responsible for our suffering? Of course not! I soon realized that they were just as innocent as we were and were doing the best they could, under the circumstances. I felt fortunate that I got to know a little about my so-called "enemies" before returning to Germany.

The almost five years I spent in Russia took away my youth. The years between seventeen and twenty-two should be very special but were robbed from me. They are lost years that can never be retrieved. But I was not alone, and there was some comfort in this thought.

So many German girls and women had been snatched from their homes, forced into hard labour for almost five years. The war was over in 1945. Why were we, mere civilians, kept prisoners until the end of 1949? This grave injustice deeply troubled me. I could not understand why this had been condoned. Perhaps this is a question that historians will grapple with someday, I thought.

Along the route to *Flensburg*, I reminded myself constantly that over half the women who were with me in those Russia prison camps did not survive. They lie buried somewhere in the Ural Mountains in Russia. I was here, on a train to *Flensburg*. I made it, I survived!

Soothed by the steady motion of the train, my thoughts explored this concept of survival. I refused to think of myself as a "victim". I had *survived* the Russian prison camps and that made me a *survivor*. At least on the physical side.

But I realized even then, that in order to survive the emotional impact of all that had happened to me, I had to learn to forgive. As strange as this may seem, I somehow understood that I had to learn to forgive the bestial actions of the Russian soldiers who had raped me. I would never survive this lingering nightmare, this other secret "aftermath" of the aftermath of the war, if I could not let go of the past.

Even though this would seem almost impossible at first, I knew I had to move beyond those ugly images of loathing and revulsion, if I wanted to live a normal life again. I must allow this concept of survival to embrace my emotional side as well. I will learn how to do this, because I am a survivor. I made that promise to myself on the train to *Flensburg* that day in 1949.

EPILOGUE

My philosophy of life was never to take good fortune for granted and I am still guided by that principle today. Another important lesson I learned in Russia was to cooperate with people to the best of my ability and to accept people as they are. This is how I would live my life, I had told myself that day on the train to *Flensburg*.

My survival in Russia and the chance to return to Germany were gifts; the greatest gifts I would ever receive and I would never take my good fortune for granted.

Flensburg was not like my childhood home in *Ostpreussen*, but it was Germany and Germany was still my country. Now, Russia and those terrible years of forced labour were finally behind me and I was looking forward to beginning a new life. A new freedom.

My Aunt Frieda was very kind to give me a home. Times were still hard in 1949, and she was struggling alone now with two children. It was November of that year when she welcomed me to her small section of an apartment she shared with another family. A tiny room of about sixteen square meters was all she had to offer me.

Aunt Frieda had a little electric stove and two beds and not much other furniture. By now, my cousin Irene was fifteen years old and her brother was already twelve years old.

One small room, shared by four people! But I had never had much room for myself as a child, and I had grown accustomed to cramped quarters in the Russian camps. I was free and I was back in my own country and that was really all that mattered to me.

There were still food shortages in Germany and Aunt Frieda had to be careful with her money. She had a small widow's pension, and worked part-time as a cook in a local school. I received a small disability cheque for a little while, because I was not considered strong enough to work full time.

I often watched Aunt Frieda cooking our dinner in her little pot and would think to myself:

"Such a little pot, so little food for four people."

It would be a long time before the feeling of hunger would go away. The gnawing in my stomach seemed to always be with me.

Even months later, I often had nightmares that I was still in Russia and that the authorities would not allow me to leave. Terrifying flashbacks of being raped, friends dying of typhoid fever, and the sinister looks of the grave-diggers would force me to relive those episodes again and again. And that terrible feeling of constant hunger accompanied me even in my dreams, along with visions of endless *kasha* and fish soups. I would awake shaking, but relieved and so thankful that I was really home at last.

I lived with my Aunt Frieda for some time and our situation slowly improved. After a few months, I found work as a health care assistant at a senior's residence, and was able to contribute to the household expenses.

Even the unbelievable nightmare of war eventually fades into the distance, I would learn. We were coping; we were learning to live normally again.

Then one day, at a special party for refugees, I met a handsome dark-haired man with piercing blue eyes, who had also been a prisoner of war in Russia. It was love at first sight for both of us, and to our surprise, we quickly learned that we had much in common. It seemed that the war and the years of imprisonment had not taken away our capacity to love. We believed we could build a future together.

A few years later, we married and would soon start a family of our own. We worked very hard, saved our money and made plans for our future.

Unfortunately I would not be re-united with Mother, Grandmother, Aunt Hanna and the rest of my *Ostpreussen* family until 1957. Thirteen years had gone by since that terrible winter of 1944!

I would learn that they had been kept in Poland after their escape from *Ostpreussen* and that the Polish authorities would not release them until 1957. So they too, were prisoners for a very long time.

In the spring of 1957, my family finally arrived in what was then called "West Germany." Unfortunately, our "family reunion" would be short and very bittersweet, because I would have to tell them that I would be leaving very soon for a new home in Canada. In fact, we would be departing for the port of Bremen just a few weeks later!

It had been our dream to eventually emigrate to Canada. My husband and I had agreed about a year earlier that there would be more opportunities for us in a land that was so hospitable to immigrants. We would set up a business and raise our family there. We were still so young, and had so many plans and dreams. Canada seemed to be a land of dreams in those days.

Once again, I would be leaving familiar surroundings. Once again, I would have to leave my *Ostpreussen* family behind, and it grieved me to do this. But this time I am making the decision, I reasoned. This time, I am not a refugee, or a prisoner of war. I am leaving so that I can make a better life for myself and for our family — in a new land.

My recently adopted home in *Flensburg* would soon be just a memory too, as my husband and I prepared for a long journey across the ocean. This journey would lead us to a new beginning, to a young country, far away from Germany. To a land as strange to me as Russia.

---

[1]This song was composed in the 1930s by Herbert Brust and became known as the *Ostpreussenlied* (English: East Prussia Song).

[2]*Ostpreussen* (English: East Prussia) had a population of over 2 million in 1939. By the end of World War II, it was reduced to about 200,000.

[3]*Pregelswalde* is known as *Saretschje (Zarec'e)* today.

[4]*Allanburg, Tapiau* and 112 other villages were part of *Wehlau.*

[5]*Königsberg* was founded in 1256 by Teutonic Knights and later became one of the largest cities and ports in Prussia. But the insanity of the Second World War would leave this once flourishing city in ruins. In a frenzy of bombings, *Königsberg*'s churches, cathedral, castle, university and shipping area were completely destroyed. Only about thirteen percent of the city's original population remained in the ruins, and this remaining population was expelled by the Soviet Union after the war. *Königsberg* was transferred to the Soviet Union in 1945, so very little remains of this city's German history and culture.

[6]*Friedland*, known as *Debrzno* was destroyed in 1945 and belongs to Poland today.

[7]After the war, *Rauschen* was transferred to the Soviet Union and became part of the *Kaliningrad Oblast.* It is now known as *Svetlogorsk.*

[8]The Red Army had cut off the escape route for thousands of fleeing East Prussians, so they were obliged to cross the frozen *Frische Haff* (English: Vistula Lagoon).

[9] *Pillau* is known as *Baltijsk* today. All German inhabitants were expelled after 1945.

[10]Bottrop is near Essen.

[11]The Red Army marched into *Bublitz* on February 27, 1945. *Bublitz* now belongs to Poland and is known as *Bobolice.*

[12] *Schlochau* is known as *Człuchów* today and belongs to Poland. The Russians reached *Schlochau* by the end of January 1945. By February 17, 1945, the city was destroyed.

Made in the USA
Coppell, TX
16 October 2021